Siri, Alexa, and Other Digital Assistants

Siri, Alexa, and Other Digital Assistants

THE LIBRARIAN'S QUICK GUIDE

Nicole Hennig

LIBRARIES UNLIMITED™

An Imprint of ABC-CLIO, LLC

Santa Barbara, California • Denver, Colorado

Library of Congress Cataloging-in-Publication Data

Names: Hennig, Nicole, author.
Title: Siri, Alexa, and other digital assistants : the librarian's quick guide / Nicole Hennig.
Description: Santa Barbara, California : Libraries Unlimited, an Imprint of ABC-CLIO, LLC, [2018] | Includes bibliographical references and index.
Identifiers: LCCN 2018030545 (print) | LCCN 2018038320 (ebook) | ISBN 9781440867262 (ebook) | ISBN 9781440867255 (paperback : alk. paper)
Subjects: LCSH: Library resources — Handbooks, manuals, etc. | Electronic reference sources — Handbooks, manuals, etc.
Classification: LCC ZA4045 (ebook) | LCC ZA4045 .H46 2018 (print) | DDC 006.3/5 — dc23
LC record available at https://lccn.loc.gov/2018030545

ISBN: 978–1–4408–6725–5 (paperback)
　　　 978–1–4408–6726–2 (ebook)

22 21 20 19 18   1 2 3 4 5

This book is also available as an eBook.

Libraries Unlimited
An Imprint of ABC-CLIO, LLC

ABC-CLIO, LLC
130 Cremona Drive, P.O. Box 1911
Santa Barbara, California 93116-1911
www.abc-clio.com

This book is printed on acid-free paper ∞

Manufactured in the United States of America

Siri is a trademark of Apple Inc., registered in the United States and other countries. Alexa and all related logos are trademarks of Amazon.com, Inc. or its affiliates. Google Assistant © 2017 Google LLC, used with permission. Google and the Google logo are registered trademarks of Google LLC.

Contents

1

What Is Voice-First Computing?

Introduction

Siri, Alexa, and Google Assistant are hot trends these days. Sales of smart speakers like Amazon Echo and Google Home are going strong, with nearly 20% of U.S. adults having access to one as of January 2018.[1] That's about 47.3 million people. The adoption rate has been stunning, reaching that number in only 2 years. It took 13 years for televisions to reach that many people and 4 years for internet access to reach the same number.[2]

Perhaps you have one of these devices and enjoy using it for basic tasks like playing music and getting weather reports. On the other hand, maybe you're one of those who say that you will never allow a listening device into your home, let alone pay to be spied on!

In this guide, you will learn about the privacy and ethical issues, as well as the benefits of voice computing. You'll look at how it's especially useful for people in hands-free situations and in the workplace and for people with vision impairments or mobility impairments. You'll look at typical tasks, the various hardware devices available, and how to create additional functionality for smart speakers (known as "skills" or "actions"). And you'll learn how this technology can be put to good use in libraries.

You may wonder why it's important for librarians to be up-to-date on voice computing. Isn't it something that's mainly for the home? Doesn't it seem unlikely that talking to computers would ever be practical in public spaces like libraries?

Actually, there are several reasons why this is an important area for librarians to become familiar with. First, experts say that voice computing is likely to be the next big revolution in computing.[3] That will affect all of us, becoming part of basic digital literacy. Second, there are many applications of voice computing for workplaces.[4] Some of those are covered in Chapter 3. And one of the most important reasons is that voice computing opens up opportunities for people with disabilities, the elderly, and people who can't easily type.[5] Since librarians care about access for all, it's important to think about how we can integrate these technologies into our services. In Chapter 3, you'll find ideas for using voice computing in libraries, including the following:

- Offering smart speakers for circulation.
- Offering smart speakers as part of accessibility workstations (perhaps in a quiet study room).
- Offering services for children and teens for learning with creative audio games and stories.
- Offering workshops on voice computing.
- Providing informational guides about voice computing, online and in print.
- Creating "Alexa skills" or "Google actions" (similar to apps) so that our users can access library services by voice.
- Offering workshops for young people and adults on how to create "skills" or "actions" for voice computing.
- Setting up a conference or study room with smart speakers, so students who are creating Alexa skills can test them.

Some libraries are already experimenting with services like these, and we'll look at some specific implementations.[6] I hope that you will feel inspired to begin experimenting with voice computing, both personally and in your library, and also that you will enjoy learning more about this technology.

Definitions

Since the advent of Amazon Echo, with its service called Alexa, various terms have emerged for this type of technology. You might hear any of the following:

- Smart digital assistants
- Voice-first devices
- Smart speakers
- Voice assistants
- Chatbots

These terms don't mean exactly the same thing. The term "chatbot" is used to describe an app that you can type questions to and get typed replies from. Instead of a live person, you are talking to a service programmed to have a "personality."[7] "Voice-first device" refers to a device (usually a speaker) that you can talk to and hear spoken replies from, like Amazon Echo or Google Home. This can get confusing because some apps, like Google Assistant on a mobile phone, offer you both options: type and talk.

For the purposes of this report, I'll use the definition provided by Alpine in their "2017 Voice Report Executive Summary": "A voice-first device is an always-on, intelligent piece of hardware where the primary interface is voice, both input and output."[8] This definition is useful because it has long been possible to talk to your mobile phone or computer (via Siri or dictation software), but Amazon Echo was the first to be *always on*, with the *primary* interface being voice. Some examples of voice-first devices are Amazon Echo, Apple's HomePod, and Google Home.

That takes care of defining the hardware, but what about the software that powers these devices? For that, we'll use the term "voice assistant." This definition from WhatIs.com is useful: "A voice assistant is a digital assistant that uses voice recognition, natural language processing and speech synthesis to provide aid to users through phones and voice recognition applications."[9] For another definition, see Amazon's developer site:[10] "The Alexa Voice Service (AVS) is Amazon's intelligent voice recognition and natural language understanding service that allows you to voice-enable any connected device that has a microphone and speaker."

Examples of voice assistants are Alexa, Google Assistant, and Siri. These services can be used to power a number of different types of devices, such as speakers, home robots, and home automation devices.

What Can Alexa Do?

In case you haven't experienced a voice-first device with its voice assistant, consider some of what Amazon's Alexa service can do. When you talk to an Alexa-enabled device like Amazon Echo, you start by saying the wake word (Alexa), so it knows you want to interact with it. You can ask it for the time, for weather reports, to play music from various music services, to answer simple questions using Wikipedia and other websites, and to control smart home devices, such as lights and your thermostat. You can also ask it for jokes, play simple games like Twenty Questions, convert units, and many other things.

A device like Amazon Echo needs to be plugged into a power outlet and set up to access your Wi-Fi network. That's because it's a cloud-based system, getting its intelligence from Amazon's services. It can't run without an internet connection (except as a Bluetooth speaker).[11] Devices like Google Home and Apple's HomePod work in much the same way. You'll find more details about those in Chapter 2.

Overview of Platforms

As of the first half of 2018, the major software platforms for voice assistants were Alexa from Amazon, Siri from Apple, Google Assistant from Google, and Cortana from Microsoft.[12] These services run on several different hardware devices, with new hardware options being released from time to time.

Here are the current voice-first devices for each platform:

Amazon's Alexa: Echo, Echo Dot, Echo Plus, Echo Spot, Echo Show, Echo Look, and the Sonos One smart speaker.[13]
Google Assistant: Google Home, Google Home Mini, Google Home Max,[14] and third-party devices like Lenovo Smart Display.[15]

Apple's Siri: HomePod.[16]
Microsoft's Cortana: Harman Kardon Invoke.[17]

There will likely be more voice-first devices available by the time you read this.[18]

Voice Assistants on Other Devices

Apple's Siri has been around for a long time and is still available on iPhone, iPad, Mac, Apple TV,[19] and Apple Watch. Similarly, voice assistants from other companies are available on other devices—Google Assistant runs on Chromecast devices, Alexa runs on Fire tablets and the Fire TV Stick, and Cortana runs on Windows computers.

There is another voice assistant from Samsung called Bixby.[20] It works on Samsung phones and will soon be integrated into smart home devices from Samsung, like the Family Hub fridge. They have plans to integrate it into TVs, washing machines, and kitchen appliances. They don't currently have a smart speaker, so it is not covered in this book.[21]

In addition, all of these major voice services run (with limited functionality) in certain mobile apps. If you're curious to try a voice assistant without having a smart speaker, you can look for these apps to use on your mobile phone. Here's a list:

- Google Assistant (Android, iOS).[22]
- Alexa: Alexa is built in to the Amazon shopping app[23] (Android, iOS), and you can also use a third-party app called Reverb[24] if you don't have an Alexa device (Android, iOS).
- Cortana (iOS, Android, Windows Phone).[25]
- Siri (iPhone, iPad, Apple Watch).[26]

Keep in mind that using these assistants via the apps usually doesn't offer all the same features available on the voice-first devices. But they are a way to get an idea of how they work.

Typical Tasks

Let's get a sense of what a smart speaker like Alexa or Google Home can do. First, it's important to know that before you talk to a smart speaker, you need to say the "wake word." This is a special word that indicates to the device that you want to ask a question or make a comment. For Amazon Echo, the default word is "Alexa."[27] If you like, you can go into the preferences on the Alexa mobile app and change the wake word to "Amazon," "Echo," or "Computer." If the idea of a microphone that's always listening bothers you, you might be relieved to know that it doesn't record anything until you say the wake word, and then it only records your question, stopping when it answers. You can delete these recordings in the mobile app if you like. Privacy issues are covered in detail in Chapter 4.

For Google Home, the wake word is either "OK Google" or "Hey Google." It will respond to either one, and the app doesn't provide a way to change the name (though some say it might in the future).[28] For Apple's HomePod, the wake word is "Hey Siri."

Here are some of the typical ways you can use your smart speaker:

- **Ask for the weather report**. Enter your address in the app first so it knows your location. Ask for the weather in other locations too, like a place you are headed for a vacation.
- **Ask for the time** (both locally and in other places).
- **Set an alarm** to wake you up or remind you of something. Choose from default tones or specific music.
- **Set timers**. This is handy when cooking. You can set multiple timers for different things, and it will keep track of all of them. You can give each timer a unique name, and you can ask how much time is left.
- **Check your calendar**. On Google Home, you can ask for information from your Google Calendar, and on Amazon Echo, you can connect calendars from Google, Microsoft, or Apple. Once you set this up in the app, you can ask what's on your calendar for the day, ask for the date of a specific event, or add appointments to your calendar. For both Google and Alexa, you can train the app with the voices of specific people in your household. This is a way to prevent people from accessing a calendar that doesn't belong to them.
- **Ask for hours and information from local businesses**. Ask about movie showtimes for theaters near you or in another location. Here are more examples: "What pharmacies are nearby?" "What's the phone number for the nearest Walgreens?"
- **Listen to music**. Most of these smart speakers connect to accounts you have on services like Spotify, Pandora, Google

Play Music, Amazon Music, and iHeartRadio. Apple's HomePod connects only to Apple Music. You can ask for a specific song, a specific artist or album, music from a certain genre, playlists you've created, and more. You can ask the speaker to increase or decrease volume, pause, stop, repeat, and more.

- **You can listen to streaming internet radio stations** from TuneIn Radio. Ask it to play a station by call letters, such as WGBH or KQED.
- **Listen to news** from sources you've selected in the app settings. Alexa calls this Flash Briefings. For example, you could choose NPR, BBC World Service, and headline news from a local news station. When you say, "Alexa, play my Flash Briefing," it will play prerecorded news from the sources you've selected.
- **Listen to podcasts**. Alexa gets its podcasts from TuneIn Radio, which has many but not all podcasts. You can say, "Alexa, play podcast Studio 360," and it will play the latest episode. There are also third-party skills (like AnyPod),[29] which you can enable for more precise control of podcasts. We'll discuss skills in a Chapter 2.
- **You can ask factual questions**, such as "What movie won the Oscar for best picture in 2018?" These smart speakers can't answer everything, but for certain basic facts, they work well. They get answers from Wikipedia and other online sources. You can find articles comparing the accuracy and usefulness of answers from Alexa, Google Assistant, and Siri.[30] Some say that Google can answer more questions because it has all of Google's search results available, but Alexa gives the answers in a more useful way, such as giving a recipe step-by-step so that you can follow it. This keeps changing as voice assistants improve, so it seems there is no clear winner for all types of questions.
- **Ask for a language translation** from English to another language. All of these devices handle basic translations, such as "How do you say 'Where is the bathroom,' in Italian?" Each platform handles different numbers of languages.
- **Use your smart speakers as a Bluetooth speaker**, sending any audio from your phone, tablet, or computer to be played on the speaker. This works on Alexa and Google Home but not on HomePod.[31] HomePod uses AirPlay to connect from other Apple devices.[32]
- **Listen to audiobooks or have your Kindle e-books read aloud**.[33] For any of your Kindle e-books, Alexa can read the text aloud and remembers where you left off when reading on other devices. For audiobooks you've purchased from Audible, you

can listen to the book on your Echo device. There are voice commands for pause, rewind, skipping between chapters, and more. With Google Home you can listen to audiobooks you've purchased on Google Play. Audiobooks from Overdrive don't have a direct connection, but you can stream them to your device via Bluetooth.[34]

- **Calls and messages**. Alexa's call and message features allow you to make and receive calls and messages between Alexa devices and apps. With Google Home, you can call by voice from your smart speaker directly to the phones of those in your contacts (Google Contacts) and local businesses (within the United States).[35]

- **There are many games available**, like Twenty Questions, Jeopardy, Myth Buster, Would You Rather?, and Rock Paper Scissors.[36] As you can imagine, verbal guessing and trivia games work well on voice-computing platforms.

- **All of these smart speakers have jokes and humor built in**. For example, say "OK Google, tell me a joke," and it will tell you one. Many of these involve puns. In my opinion, the jokes from Google are funnier than those from Alexa. That could be because they've hired writers from Pixar and The Onion.[37] In addition, the engineers of these systems have built in some fun "Easter eggs" or hidden humorous responses that you often find by accident.[38] These usually involve popular culture, for example, "Alexa, who you gonna call?" or "OK Google, where's Waldo?" or "Hey Siri, can you stop time?"

- **Control smart home devices**. With smart speakers, you can control home automation devices like lights, thermostats, garage doors, security alarms, video doorbells, smart plugs for any device, and many more.[39] Many devices work with more than one platform from Amazon, Google, and Apple.[40]

- **Activate tasks in other apps with your voice**. There is a service called IFTTT (If This, Then That) that connects different apps together so that when something happens in one app, it triggers an action in another app. These are called IFTTT applets. One nice feature is that IFTTT offers a number of different applets for voice assistants.[41] For example, you can create a note in Evernote by speaking to Google Assistant,[42] or you can tell Alexa to email your shopping list to you (the one you've created by voice with Alexa).[43]

This is not a complete list of what these devices can do but is meant only as an introduction. You'll look at more capabilities in the next section about third-party skills.

Third-Party Skills

In addition to the standard abilities that smart speakers have, most of these platforms allow third-party developers to create additional functionality.[44] Amazon was the first to do this, and they called these "skills." Google followed, calling these "actions."

Alexa Skills

Alexa has the most skills by far, over 30,000 at the time of this writing. New skills are being developed all the time, and the number is growing quickly, increasing from just over 5,000 skills in 2016 to over 30,000 by March 2018.[45] There are a wide variety of skills available. You can browse them on Amazon's website in the menu option Alexa Skills, or in the Alexa app on your mobile device, under Skills. There are skills for everything from calling an Uber to reading a customized bedtime story to your child.

Skills are available in the following categories:

- Business and finance
- Communication
- Connected car
- Education and reference
- Food and drink
- Games, trivia, and accessories
- Health and fitness
- Home services
- Kids
- Lifestyle
- Local
- Movies and TV
- Music and audio
- News
- Novelty and humor
- Productivity
- Shopping
- Smart home
- Social
- Sports
- Travel and transportation

- Utilities
- Weather

Here are some examples of skills so you can get an idea of the breadth of what's available:

1. **Stories** — Short Bedtime Story.[46] "Alexa, tell bedtime story to Allie." With this skill, you can tell Alexa the name of your child, and the story will be personalized with your child's name. There are several stories available.
2. **Games**[47] — There are many games available, like Rock Paper Scissors, Jeopardy, Would You Rather, and Twenty Questions. It makes sense that games like these translate well to a spoken environment.
3. **Adventure games** — The Magic Door.[48] This skill is an interactive "choose your own adventure" game with original stories. You explore a magical land with various regions and creatures.
4. **Facts** — There are many skills that tell you interesting facts. One of my favorites is Black History Facts.[49] It's designed well and uses actors' voices instead of just Alexa's own voice.
5. **Travel** — Flight Tracker.[50] You can ask questions like "Alexa, ask Flight Tracker, has LH1060 arrived?" or "Alexa, ask Flight Tracker, where is LX155?" To research flight options, get the Kayak skill.[51]
6. **Banking** — CapitalOne.[52] "Alexa, ask CapitalOne, what's my balance?" In this banking skill, you can ask for your balance, pay your credit card bill, find out how much you spent at a particular vendor last week, and exercise many more options. Of course, you have to authenticate this with your bank first, and not many banks offer this at the time of this writing, but it's likely that more will do so in the future.
7. **First aid** — Mayo Clinic First Aid.[53] Ask questions like "Help for a burn" or "Tell me about spider bites." It's handy to use voice computing when you might have an injury and can't so easily type on your computer or touch your phone.
8. **Physical fitness** — Five Minute Workout: Core and Cardio.[54] There are many workout and yoga skills that guide you through a routine by voice.
9. **Nature** — Bird Song.[55] Learn about bird calls in this skill. Ask for a specific bird, "Alexa, ask Bird Song for a blackbird," or listen to a continuous stream of bird songs, "Alexa, ask Bird Song for a song stream." There is also a game included where you can guess which bird you're hearing.

10. **Science**—NASA Mars.[56] Learn about Mars in this skill from NASA. For example, "Alexa, ask NASA Mars, what Curiosity is doing on Mars?" or "Alexa, ask NASA Mars why is Mars red?" There are many other science skills. With Astronomy Guide[57] you can ask, "Alexa, ask Astronomy Guide for seeing conditions near Madison, Wisconsin," "Alexa, ask Astronomy Guide for observing highlights in March," or "Alexa, ask Astronomy Guide which planets are visible in June?"

11. **Personal alerts**—Ask My Buddy[58] is a valuable skill for alerting your friends or family members if you have fallen or need help and can't get to your phone. You set up your alert network in advance, and the skill can send text messages, emails, or phone calls to your designated persons. For example, say, "Alexa, Ask My Buddy to alert 'Your Contact' " or "Alexa, Ask My Buddy to alert everyone." This service will send an alert so people in your alert network can check on you. It's not a substitute for 911 service but can be very useful in certain situations. See a video demo here: https://youtu.be/rX46MC26T_E.

12. **Food and cooking**—Love and Lemons.[59] There are many food and cooking skills. This one allows you to browse and make recipes from the Love and Lemons whole-food-based cooking blog. Follow along with recipes step by step; pause and resume as needed. For example, "Alexa, ask Love and Lemons to read me the ingredients one by one."

13. **Cars**—My Tesla (Unofficial).[60] With this skill, you can get information about your Tesla car, such as how much charge is left on the battery, the vehicle's location, and climate status. You can send commands, such as warm up the car, flash the lights, honk, and start or stop charging. If you don't have a Tesla, try the skill by Automatic, with its $100 gadget that plugs into your car's onboard diagnostic port to show you statistics about your driving.[61]

In addition to these examples, there are skills for converting currencies, doing math, making measurements, ordering products, organizing shopping lists, controlling your television, getting travel information, and much more.[62]

You can ask Alexa for any particular skill if you know its name, or you can ask her to recommend skills for a topic or tell you about the top skills in a category. In addition, there is a skill called Skill Finder.[63] This offers more detailed commands for finding new skills to try.

Google Actions

Google calls their added functionality "actions." For a directory of actions, see https://assistant.google.com/explore/. Another way to browse a directory is in the Assistant app on your mobile device. Tap the icon in the upper right to go to the Explore screen. Here you can search by name or explore categories, which include the following:

- Arts and lifestyle
- Business and finance
- Education and reference
- Food and drink
- Games and fun
- Health and fitness
- Home control
- Kids and family
- Local
- Movies, photos, and TV
- Music and audio
- News and magazines
- Productivity
- Shopping
- Social and communication
- Sports
- Travel and transportation
- Weather

In Google, to use an action, you say, "OK Google, talk to [name of the action]." For example, say, "OK Google, talk to Time Machine." This is an action that tells you historical facts from 1851 to the present that happened on the same day in a previous year.

Like Alexa skills, there are many different actions. To see a list of some recommended ones, see "50 Best Google Assistant Skills and Actions" at https://beebom.com/best-google-assistant-skills-actions/. As of early 2018, there were nearly 2,000 Google actions (as opposed to over 30,000 Alexa skills).[64]

Third-Party Apps for Siri on HomePod

Siri on HomePod works well for the usual tasks, like playing music, listening to podcasts, setting alarms and timers, getting weather forecasts, converting units, translation, traffic, general knowledge, and home automation.

But for third-party apps, there is limited support. Instead of running tasks in the cloud like Amazon and Google, Siri on HomePod hands off certain tasks to your nearby iPhone or iPad.[65] For example, you can dictate text messages, and HomePod hands the task off to your iPhone.

For apps by third-party developers, Siri on HomePod currently works only with three categories: messaging, lists, and notes. The developers of these apps need to support Apple's SiriKit[66] in order to make them work with HomePod.

This means you can say, "Hey Siri, add do yoga to my to-do list in Things" or "Hey Siri, send a message to Maria with WhatsApp." Siri on HomePod also works with apps like Evernote, Things, and Remember the Milk for dictating notes, to-do lists, and reminders. One hopes that eventually, Apple will make this available to other types of apps so more of them can be controlled by voice with HomePod.

Amazon Remains in the Lead

Amazon's Alexa had a huge head start by coming out two years before Google Assistant and a little more than three years ahead of Siri on HomePod. By opening the creation of skills to third-party developers, they took the lead in the number of skills. This doesn't always mean that all the skills are of high quality, and it can be difficult to learn new skills and remember what they are called in order to use them. But it's interesting to see what kinds of creative tasks developers are enabling with their skills. We'll discuss skill creation in Chapter 2, including why you might want to create a skill, what tools you can use, and whether it's possible to monetize your skill.

Statistics

People are quickly adopting smart speakers. Statistics from the 2018 Infinite Dial study[67] show that the adoption rate is growing even more quickly than the adoption rate during the early days of smartphones.[68] Gartner Research predicts that "by 2020, 30 percent of web browsing sessions will be done without a screen" because of voice-first computing.[69]

According to a study from Edison Research at the end of 2017, Amazon Echo had the major market share for smart speakers at 69% of the market. Google Home had 25% and other speakers 6%. This is not surprising since Amazon Echo came out two years before other smart speakers. But it's interesting to see that Google Home is gaining share over time. Its market share is expected to grow and maybe even overtake Amazon Echo at some point.[70] Loup Ventures predicts that Google Home will overtake Alexa by 2022 with 48% of the market, with Alexa at 37%, Apple's HomePod at 12%, and others at 3%.[71]

The 2017 *Smart Audio Report* from NPR and Edison Research[72] provides interesting statistics about how people use these devices. Here are some points from the study:

- Sixteen percent of Americans over 18 own a smart speaker (about 39 million people).
- Sixty-five percent of survey respondents say they wouldn't want to go back to life without their smart speaker.
- Thirty-nine percent of people owning smart speakers say it's replacing time spent with traditional AM/FM radio. Thirty-four percent say it replaces time with smartphones, and 30% say it replaces time with television.
- It's not a solitary activity. When they are asked, "How often do you use the smart speaker with others in your household?" 53% say, "Most of the time," and 39% say, "Occasionally."
- The top tasks people do together with friends and family are playing music (60%), asking a general question (30%), and getting the weather report (28%).

Edison Research together with NPR conducts recurring studies about smart speaker ownership and usage; you can look for their most current report at https://www.nationalpublicmedia.com/smart-audio-report/. These reports are always very interesting.

Another interesting report that comes out periodically is *The Infinite Dial Study* by Edison Research and Triton Digital.[73] It covers usage of smart speakers in addition to other topics, such as the use of digital audio and podcast consumption. The following are some interesting points from this report:[74]

- How many smart speakers do people have in a household? Sixty-seven percent said one, 22% two, and 11% three or more.
- Seventy-two percent own Amazon Alexa but not Google Home, 17% own Google Home but not Alexa, and 11% own both.

As the prices come down, people will likely continue to have more than one of these devices at home, sometimes from multiple platforms. Echo Dot and Google Home Mini are usually priced at $49, and they sometimes go on sale for $10 or $20 off. These low-cost devices have the same capabilities as the full-sized products, without a high-quality speaker built in. (You can use them with external speakers.) Other inexpensive options are appearing, like the Eufy Genie Smart Speaker with Amazon Alexa for $35.[75] With prices like these, people can put one in every room. It seems likely that voice computing will continue to grow at a rapid pace.

Advantages of Voice Computing

While voice computing is not appropriate for all situations, for certain ones it's very useful. Think of times when your hands are busy, wet, or dirty. And think of how much faster it is to talk than to type. There are studies showing that talking to a mobile device can be three times faster than typing.[76] Voice computing can be more practical and safer than typing in many situations, like during food preparation, taking care of infants and young children, and while driving.

Voice computing is also more intuitive because everyone knows how to talk. You don't need to learn a system of menus or commands; you can just ask for something. When a voice assistant replies, the tone of voice can convey information that words on a screen can't easily do. For example, when you ask Google Home for a joke, it raises its voice and says, "This might make you laugh," and proceeds to tell the joke in a happy, somewhat silly tone of voice.

Not every situation is best served by voice, though. Designers like Cathy Pearl advise app developers to consider whether a voice interface makes sense for their particular task, rather than jumping on the bandwagon because voice computing is trendy. She advises against voice for situations where talking would be disruptive, like in open-plan offices.[77] Some people just don't feel comfortable talking to computers. Others already spend most of their time texting and may not want to switch modes. And most important is privacy. People don't want to discuss health issues out loud while riding the train to work. It can be a real privacy violation for a voice assistant to read your prescription information out loud or remind you to take a medication in situations where others can hear.

So even though voice is not best for every situation, when it makes sense, it's extremely useful. One of the greatest benefits of voice computing is that it removes barriers for people with visual impairments or physical disabilities. We'll look at several examples of this in upcoming chapters. As this area matures, we'll likely see combination interfaces, making the best use of voice commands together with typing, touch, and visual displays, in ways that are most appropriate for the situation.

2

Hardware and Skills

Smart Speakers

Now let's look at a selection of voice-first devices, beginning with smart speakers. As previously noted, Amazon took the lead in this area, releasing Amazon Echo in November 2014. Google Home was released in November 2016, Harman Kardon Invoke with Cortana came out in October 2017, and Apple's HomePod came out in February 2018.

Amazon Alexa Devices

Amazon has several smart speaker models, so many that it can be hard to keep up with which one is which! They tend to experiment with new ideas and release new models from time to time. Here is a list of available models as of this writing:

- **Amazon Echo (2nd generation).**[1] This is the newest version of their most basic smart speaker. It comes in several different colors and finishes.
- **Echo Dot (2nd generation).**[2] This is their smaller, less expensive model, designed to be used with an external speaker, either with an audio cable or via Bluetooth. It has the same capabilities as Amazon Echo, just without the higher-quality speaker built in.
- **Echo Dot (Kids Edition).**[3] This is a version of Echo Dot that comes with Amazon FreeTime on Alexa, a version of Alexa

built with kids in mind. It includes parental controls for filtering explicit songs, disabling voice purchasing, pausing it during dinner or homework time, and setting bedtime limits. It comes with a kid-friendly case in red, green, or blue along with a guarantee for two years, in case your child breaks it. It also includes a one-year free trial of FreeTime Unlimited for access to more educational content like children's audiobooks, children's games, ad-free radio stations, and skills designed for kids.

- **Echo Show**.[4] This model includes a screen (seven inches diagonally) so you can get some of your results visually. You can watch video flash briefings for news; see your to-do lists and shopping lists; see lyrics on screen with Amazon Music; make video calls to family and friends who also have Echo Show, Echo Spot, or the Alexa app on their phone; monitor your security camera or baby monitor (with compatible devices); and watch videos from Vimeo, Dailymotion, and Amazon Prime Video (but not YouTube, due to a dispute between Google and Amazon).[5]
- **Echo Spot**.[6] The Spot is a small, cute, round model with a 2.5-inch screen that many people use on their bedside table as a smart alarm clock.[7] It has the same features as the Show but in a smaller package, with a smaller speaker (1.4-inch speaker instead of the dual 2.0-inch speakers found in the Show).
- **Echo Plus with built-in hub**.[8] This model is the same as the Echo but with a built-in smart home hub. The hub allows for easy setup of compatible smart home devices. The addition of the hub makes it taller than the Echo, at 9.3 inches tall instead of 5.9 inches.
- **Echo Look**.[9] This model is specifically geared to clothing and fashion. It includes a camera for taking full-length photos and short videos of you in different outfits, in order to give you advice on what to wear. It's currently only available by invitation but may be available to anyone by the time you read this. It can catalog your outfits in a "look book" and make fashion recommendations using machine learning. Of course, it has a shopping function, making it easy to buy clothing from Amazon.[10] It may also prove helpful to blind people since they often need advice on what clothing goes together.[11]
- **Amazon Tap**.[12] The Tap is Amazon's portable Bluetooth speaker designed for listening to music and other audio on the go. It's meant to be taken with you to a friend's house or to the beach so you can listen to music. You can connect your phone, tablet, or computer via an audio cable or via Bluetooth. It is said to run about nine hours on its battery charge. If you connect it to

Wi-Fi, it can play streaming music from the usual services (Spotify, Pandora, etc.). In order to use Alexa's features, you need to tap a button to wake it up before you talk to it. That's why it's called Tap. It's set up this way in order to save battery life since having the microphone on all the time uses more power. (There is a setting in the Alexa app that you can turn on to have the microphone always listening. Go to Settings and select Hands-Free. However, turning this on will deplete the battery faster.) Since it's designed primarily as a speaker, it has better sound quality than the Echo. It uses dual-stereo speakers with Dolby processing.

- **Fire tablet with Alexa.**[13] This tablet includes the ability to use Alexa to ask questions, play music, check your calendar, and perform other typical Alexa tasks. You need to push the home button in order for the microphone to listen. You can also use the calling and messaging features with people who have other Alexa devices. It comes in various sizes, and there is also a kids' edition.

Google Home Devices

Google Home has three models as of this writing: the original Google Home, a smaller version called Google Home Mini, and a larger version called Google Home Max.

- **Google Home.**[14] This smart speaker was released in late 2016. It has the same capabilities as Amazon Echo. It has a pleasing size and shape, in white with a gray fabric base. You can customize it by purchasing a base in different colors. The base connects with magnets, so it's easy to remove the original one to install others. You can also install third-party skins to customize the appearance of the top.[15]
- **Google Home Mini.**[16] This smaller version is similar to Echo Dot. It's cheaper than the standard Google Home, with lower quality sound. Unlike Echo Dot, it has no line-out for plugging into an external speaker. Neither can you connect a device to it via Bluetooth (as you can with Google Home). Instead, you need a Chromecast Audio device to connect to your existing speakers.[17] This will allow you to "cast" music from your smartphone, tablet, or computer.
- **Google Home Max.**[18] This is Google's high-end option, with an integrated speaker system. It has dual high-excursion woofers and two custom tweeters. According to Google, it uses

machine learning to automatically adjust the equalizer settings to match the acoustics of the room it's in.

As of early 2018, several companies are beginning to announce products with Google Assistant built in.[19] One example that looks promising is Lenovo Smart Display. It will be similar to Echo Show, with a screen for displaying visual results.[20]

Apple's HomePod

Apple's HomePod was released in February 2018 to mixed reviews. Reviewers agreed about the great sound quality,[21] but most found the implementation of Siri to be lacking compared to Alexa or Google Home.[22] It's a cylinder-shaped speaker, 6.8 inches by 5.6 inches, available in either black or white. There is a touchscreen on top with a swirling LED light that shows whenever the device is speaking or listening. Reviewers praise it for its ability to hear voices, even from around corners, with loud music playing, and with other noises in the background. It has an array of six microphones inside for capturing your voice. It works with Apple Music but not other music services (as of this writing). You need an iPhone to set it up, so Android users are out of luck. You can use AirPlay to stream audio content from your iPhone, iPad, Mac, or Apple TV. AirPlay is a way to play content from other services like Spotify or YouTube, but you lack voice control for rewind, pause, and other features with this method.

One of the best features of the HomePod is that it has great sound quality anywhere you place it. It has seven tweeters arrayed in a circle and a four-inch woofer pointing out of the top. The six microphones not only hear your voice but also help sample the proximity of nearby walls and ceilings. This allows it to change how it's sending out the music for best sound quality, depending on where you put it, and changing dynamically when you move it to a different location.

According to Apple, "When against a wall or on a bookshelf, the A8 chip analyzes the music and appropriately beams direct energy and center vocals into the middle of the room, while reflecting the ambient reverb and backup vocals against the wall for dispersion in the room."[23]

As for Siri on HomePod, it works to play music, listen to podcasts, get the weather, set alarms and timers, and perform unit conversions and math and other general knowledge tasks. You can use HomePod to control your smart home devices, and those need to be HomeKit enabled.[24]

HomePod is designed as a single-user device. The person in your family who sets it up is the one whose Apple Music account is used. Any reminders, notes, or messages sent are from that person's account. This is different than devices from Amazon and Google; on Amazon and Google devices, you can set up multiple users so different voices can be recognized.

As of this writing, most reviewers agree that HomePod is great for sound quality and works best if you have Apple Music and Apple devices. It's likely that more features will be added over the next year or so, enabling more tasks and hopefully multiuser accounts. Some reviewers suggest that the best improvements would be to make it work more completely as a hub for all your Apple devices and tasks.[25]

Microsoft Cortana—Harman Kardon Invoke

Microsoft's Cortana is available in a smart speaker, but many people haven't heard about this. It's the Invoke, by Harman Kardon. It gets positive reviews for sound quality but negative reviews for the capabilities of Cortana.[26]

It's a nice-looking smart speaker, with a tapered cylindrical shape. It comes in either black or silver. It has a button for turning the microphone on or off and a Bluetooth pairing button on the back. You can say, "Hey Cortana," or touch the top panel to make her listen to you. It has excellent sound quality, with three woofers, three tweeters, two passive radiators, and an amplifier. Its sound can fill a room quite easily.

It has seven far-field microphones designed to pick up your voice from far away or in the next room, but reviewers say that it doesn't hear them very well unless they speak loudly in the same room.

Like other smart speakers, you can ask Cortana for simple facts, set timers and alarms, and get the news. It integrates with Outlook.com and Office 365 for checking meetings on your calendar. Other services it connects with are Skype (for hands-free calling), LinkedIn, and Wunderlist. For playing music, it connects to

Spotify, iHeartRadio, and TuneIn. Microsoft says it will add more music options soon, like Pandora and possibly SoundCloud. To set it up, you use the Cortana app on a Windows PC or on your iPhone or Android phone. Most reviews of it at this point agree that the sound quality is excellent, but its capabilities just don't measure up to other smart speakers.[27]

Smart Home Devices

One of the features people like most about smart speakers is the ability to enable control of smart home devices with your voice. At this point, there are many types of smart home devices from many different manufacturers. You can get smart bulbs (which change colors), dimmers and light switches, smart plugs and wall outlets (so you can plug in appliances to turn on by voice), thermostats, robotic vacuums, security cameras, door locks, doorbell cameras, ceiling fans, baby monitors, carbon monoxide detectors, garage door controllers, sprinkler controllers, kitchen appliances, and more.[28]

Some devices work with only Apple's HomeKit platform, and others only with Alexa or with Google. If you might want to use smart speakers from different platforms, it's a good idea to get devices that work with multiple platforms. It's easy to find articles that recommend these—for example, "Alexa? HomeKit? Google Home? These Gizmos Work with All Three."[29]

We'll discuss some of the privacy and security issues of smart home devices in Chapter 4. In the meantime, know that smart homes are here, with new features and devices coming out frequently.

TV Devices

The ability to control your TV with your voice is here, but it's not as useful as one would hope. You can do some useful things, like turn on the TV and ask for a specific Netflix show, but you can't do everything easily by voice, such as browse through listings and choose a specific episode of a show. For some functions, it's easier to use buttons on a remote.

There are several different options for voice control of your TV. Here are the primary ones:

- Siri with Apple TV using Siri Remote.[30]
- Google Assistant with Chromecast.[31]
- Alexa with Amazon Fire TV or TV Stick with voice remote.[32] Speak to Alexa on the voice remote, or pair an Echo device in your home to a particular Fire TV for voice control without a remote.[33]
- Alexa with Logitech Harmony Hub.[34]
- Some set-top boxes and satellite receivers offer voice control with Alexa, such as Dish Hopper DVR/set-top box and Wally satellite receiver.[35]

Some television manufacturers are starting to include Alexa or Google voice control in the TV itself. Sony, Hisense, and LG have announced integration with Alexa in some of their new TVs.[36] Sony and LG have announced the same for Google Assistant.[37]

Some typical things you can do are as follows:

- Turn on the TV.
- Launch a movie or TV show.
- Pause, play, rewind, and fast-forward.
- Jump forward or back a certain amount of time.
- Skip to next or previous episode.
- Turn on or off closed captions (Google Chromecast and Siri).
- Adjust the volume.
- Search and browse through listings (Alexa and Siri, not Google Chromecast).
- Conduct detailed searches and refine them (Siri).[38]

For a complete list of commands for controlling TV, see the following:

- "Use Your Alexa Device to Control Your Fire TV," https://www.amazon.com/gp/help/customer/display.html?nodeId=202174250.
- "Use Siri on Your Apple TV 4K or Apple TV (4th Generation)," https://support.apple.com/en-us/HT205300.
- "Play TV Shows & Movies Using Google Home," https://support.google.com/googlehome/answer/7214982?hl=en.

Each voice assistant platform works with different streaming media services, because of licensing agreements and disputes between Google and Amazon. For example:

- Alexa offers voice control with Amazon Prime Video and also for launching specific apps like Netflix, Hulu, and HBO Now. You need to connect your accounts in advance, using the mobile app. Google has pulled the YouTube app from Fire TV,[39] but there is a work-around involved using a built-in web browser on the Fire TV to access it.[40] This may change as Amazon and Google continue their negotiations.
- Google Assistant works with YouTube, Netflix, Hulu, and others but not directly with Amazon Prime Video. As with Alexa, you will need to connect your accounts in advance, using the mobile app. There is a work-around, though—you can "cast" from your computer using a Chrome browser to the Chromecast-connected TV to show content from your Amazon Prime Video account.[41]
- Siri on Apple TV works with video content from iTunes (unlike Alexa or Google Assistant). It also works with Amazon Prime Video, YouTube, and the usual streaming services via apps, such as Netflix, Hulu, and HBO Now.

In addition, most of these voice-controlled TV devices offer the ability to ask for weather reports, get sports scores, play music, display your photos, ask trivia questions, listen to streaming radio, listen to audiobooks, and perform other tasks that smart speakers can do.[42]

In future, hopefully you won't always need to use a remote control with these devices but instead can just talk to your digital assistant, whether it's located in a smart speaker, a smart TV, or a media streamer box. This might offer the best of both worlds (seeing results on a screen and voice control). We are beginning to see this merging of visuals and voice with devices like Echo Show.[43]

In addition to smart speakers and smart TVs, there are a number of other devices that use voice computing. Home robots, smart speakers in cars, and "hearables" are some of the most interesting examples.

Home Robots

A few examples of home robots are Jibo,[44] Kuri,[45] and Sony's Aibo (a robot puppy).[46] They are designed to move around your house and do tasks such as give weather reports, set alarms, take photos, control smart home devices, and play music. These robots are designed to have cute personalities that make people laugh and enjoy interacting with them. Since these are very early versions of home robots, they generally get good reviews for how fun and cute they are but not so good reviews for what tasks they can accomplish compared to Alexa or Google Home.[47] It will be interesting to see how these robots improve over time.

Jibo's founder and chief scientist is Cynthia Breazeal, a professor at Massachusetts Institute of Technology (MIT). She aims to build robots that help encourage family interaction (rather than isolating people like smartphones sometimes do). She also aims to build products that encourage a growth mind-set in children.[48] To help with that vision, her company has released a companion app called Be a Maker.[49] This app is designed for kids ages 7–12 and makes it easy to program Jibo to do fun things, such as dance, tell jokes, take photos, and say the names of specific people. It's based on the open-source programming language for kids called Scratch (developed at MIT). You can see a demo of it on YouTube: https://youtu .be/AO1q4mtXPLc. Learning to program robots is a fun way for kids to learn logic and problem solving.

As of this writing, home robots are significantly more expensive than smart speakers. For example, you can order an Amazon Echo for about $90, while a Jibo costs about $900. As with most new technologies, you can expect the prices to come down and the technology to improve.

To get a sense of what's coming in future, it's worth looking at video examples of several of these robots, such as Sony's Aibo (robot puppy) (https://aibo.sony.jp/en/), Jibo (https://youtu.be/ 37dAP2D0rqc), and Kuri home robot (https://www.heykuri.com/ explore-kuri/#feature-cap-touch-sensors).

Voice Computing in Cars

Services like Alexa and Google Assistant are coming to cars. Some manufacturers are already building them into cars,[50] but if your car doesn't have voice computing, you can purchase stand-alone devices[51] to add it. In addition, Google Assistant is available in Android Auto (available in many makes of cars).[52]

An advantage of this is that voice computing removes the distraction of looking down at your phone for directions or to change a music playlist. Now you can tell your car to give you directions, send a text message, make a call, play your favorite music, help you find nearby gas stations, and order food to be delivered as you arrive home — all without looking at any screens.

There are also Alexa skills that work with a connected car adapter to let you monitor your gas mileage, remember where you parked, and alert you of potential maintenance issues.[53] A popular one is Automatic Pro.[54] It can even automatically call 911 if you've been in an accident.[55]

If you've gotten used to voice computing at home, you'll likely find that you wish you could use it while driving — maybe you've even tried to talk to your car radio. Some people have put a simple Echo Dot in their car to use this way (if their car has Wi-Fi).[56] It seems likely that this will be standard in most cars in the not-so-distant future.

Hearables

According to the site Everyday Hearing,

> A hearable is a wireless in-ear computational earpiece. Essentially you have a microcomputer that fits in your ear canal and utilizes wireless technology to supplement and enhance your listening experience.[57]

This category known as "hearables" includes smart hearing aids, personal sound amplifiers, augmented hearing, and personal headphones. Many of these devices are coming out with voice assistant capabilities built in.

Here are a few examples of wireless earbuds with voice assistant capabilities. Apple's AirPods integrate with Siri and can be activated by tapping on one of the earbuds. A new model to be released in late 2018 or early 2019 will include the ability to activate by saying "Hey Siri" without touching the earbuds.[58] Another option is from Jabra. They offer Elite 65t and Elite Active 65t wireless earbuds that integrate with Alexa, Siri, and Google Assistant. The included app lets you choose which voice assistant you prefer to use.[59] In October 2017, Google released Pixel Buds that integrate with Google Assistant, but it has received mostly negative reviews.[60] Hopefully, a future release will improve this product because its feature for translating languages on the fly in near real time has many people excited about breaking down language barriers.[61]

This area is rapidly growing and is something to watch, as people find voice computing in the ear to be very convenient for certain situations. One more company worth mentioning is SmartEar.ai.[62] They are working on a hearable device that is comfortable for wearing all day, manages your auditory environment, connects you to an intelligent assistant through voice, and monitors your health and fitness. It's worth watching the video on their home page for a vision of what it will do: https://www.smartear.ai/.

If you've seen the movie *Her*, where the main character (played by Joaquin Phoenix) falls in love with the playful, intelligent voice assistant in his ear (played by Scarlett Johansson), you'll see an imagined future where people wear computers in their ear most of the time.[63] It seems we are headed in this direction with some of these products.

Comparing Platforms

With all of these options for voice-first devices, it can be hard to decide which platform to use. There are many comparison articles discussing differences, and some of these include a list of questions for testing each platform to compare how well they perform.[64]

Some reviewers say Alexa is best because it has been around the longest, has the most third-party skills, and makes it easiest to set up smart home devices using the model that includes a hub.[65] Others say Google Assistant is best because Google has access to all of Google's artificial intelligence technology, so it can theoretically be better at answering questions. And finally, Siri on HomePod gets praise for being the best-sounding speaker and a good choice for those who use Apple devices. Microsoft's Cortana is widely agreed to be far behind, so it isn't usually included in comparison reviews at this time.

Changes to these platforms come quickly. One day Alexa will have features that Google doesn't, and the next day Google adds those features (the ability to read audiobooks, for example). Sometimes Google is first, such as when they provided calendar access by voice for different people in a household. Alexa added the ability to recognize multiple voices soon after.

Another thing to consider is that many smart home devices work with multiple platforms, so that's good news. You can switch platforms or use multiple ones in the same household. In fact, it can be fun to have different devices (an Amazon Echo and a Google Home, for example), because they each seem to have a different personality, tone of voice, and sense of humor. The only downside to having both is that you sometimes call them by the wrong name (just like children), saying "Alexa," when you meant to say "Hey Google."

If you are thinking of getting these for your library to experiment with, consider getting an Amazon Echo *and* a Google Home. That way you can learn about two of the leading platforms. You could put these in a conference or study room for people to try in the library, or you could offer them to loan out, as the Framingham Public Library does.[66] You'll learn more about how libraries are using these devices in Chapter 3.

Creating Skills

Alexa Skill Development

In Chapter 1, you learned about the rapidly growing set of third-party skills for Alexa—over 30,000 skills as of March 2018. You might want to try your hand at creating a skill, either for the general public or for your library users.

Luckily, skill creation is not very difficult. There is some coding involved, so it's good to have some basic coding knowledge, but there are many templates available to easily modify. There are even tools available that make it easy to create skills without coding.[67]

It's worth noting that the processing of natural language is done by Amazon on their servers. Your code only needs to provide information about what Alexa should listen for and how she should respond. There are many tutorials available online that walk you through the process.[68] When you build a skill, you need to write the code and host it somewhere. Amazon provides a service called AWS Lambda, and you can host your code there if you prefer not to host it on your own servers. You then need to create an account on Amazon's Developer Services Portal. You add your skill there and point it to the place where your code is hosted. You'll need to sign up for an Amazon Developer account in order to begin creating your skill. Refer to the Alexa Skills Kit for the documentation.[69]

One of the easiest types of skills to start with is a fact skill. These are skills where you ask Alexa for a random fact based on a topic (e.g., Black History Facts[70] or Human Body Facts[71]). You need to think about how people might phrase questions and responses so you can include lists of what to listen for. You can connect your skill to third-party databases using sources online that have an application programming interface (API). A good place to start learning is Amazon's "Fact Skill Tutorial: Build an Alexa Skill in 6 Steps," which you can find at https://developer.amazon.com/alexa-skills-kit/tutorials/fact-skill-1.

If you'd like to learn more about how this works, you might enjoy reading articles by some of the people who've already created skills. These two are recommended: Lorrie Pearson's "How I Programmed My First Amazon Alexa Skill and Won a Free Echo Dot"[72] and Hugh Langley's "What It's Like to Build an Alexa Skill—and How You Can Do It Yourself."[73]

Once you've created your skill, you need to submit it to Amazon for review. They will look for bugs, security issues, and also at your content to make sure it complies with their policies on privacy and other issues. They usually approve skills in three to seven days.

If you'd like to try creating a skill without coding, take a look at Storyline, a prototyping tool: https://getstoryline.com/. You can sign up for a free account and use their drag and drop interface to build your voice interactions. They offer video tutorials to walk you through the process. They also make it easy to submit your skill to Amazon. Even if you do want to write your own code, this can be a useful prototyping tool to help you focus on what you want to build before you code it. There is another prototyping tool called Sayspring[74] that focuses on the design and prototyping of skills, without generating code for you to submit. This is a useful tool if you want to create a prototype to give to someone else to code. Both Storyline and Sayspring offer free accounts so you can try them out before deciding if you want to pay for more features.[75]

The Westport Library, a public library in Westport, Connecticut, offers workshops for their users on building Alexa skills. See http:// westportlibrary.org/events/amazon-alexa-skills-bootcamp.

Google Action Development

Like Amazon, Google offers a way for developers to create what they call "actions."[76] It's fairly simple, and there are many good tutorials online.[77] They offer prizes up to $10,000 to developers who win their developer challenge.[78] You can read about the 2017 winners in Bret Kinsella's "Voice App '100 Years Ago' Wins Actions on Google Developer Challenge," Voicebot.AI, December 11, 2017, https://www.voicebot.ai/2017/12/11/voice-app-100-years-ago-wins -actions-google-developer-challenge/.

Is It Possible to Monetize a Skill?

Most Alexa skills these days are free. Amazon doesn't allow most skill developers to charge or serve ads. Most developers create these as a hobby or as a way to learn about a rapidly growing area that may pay off in the future.

A few lucky developers make money through Amazon's Alexa Developer Rewards program.[79] For certain categories of skills,[80] Amazon selects the ones with high levels of use and sends payment to those developers.

Another way that developers make money is by creating skills for major brands to help them market their products. You can find a list of agencies that do this on Amazon's site: https://developer .amazon.com/alexa/agencies-and-tools.

Amazon is still experimenting with ways to monetize skills.[81] It now offers in-skill purchasing, making it possible to sell digital sub- scriptions or premium content in a skill. Sony made the Jeopardy skill, and they offer subscriptions to Double Jeopardy for getting more clues. Amazon Pay is another way to make money; in certain skills people can pay for food delivery through a voice skill.[82]

Amazon also hosts Alexa Prize, a competition for college and university teams to win money for building creative skills. They are evaluated on technical merit, the novelty of their idea, potential contributions to the field of voice interfaces, and each team's execution of their plan. Winners receive a research grant of $250,000, a free Amazon Web Services account, Alexa devices, and support for their team. To read an interesting story of several teams competing for this prize, see James Vlahos's "Inside the Alexa Prize," *Wired*, February 27, 2018, https://www.wired.com/story/inside-amazon-alexa-prize/.

Creating Skills for Libraries

If you've read this far, you're probably thinking about ideas for skills that libraries could create—perhaps a skill for asking your public library about events, when your items are due, or putting items on hold. Maybe you'd like to create a skill for academic libraries where students can search for a particular article by voice or reserve a study room.

In Chapter 3, you'll explore these ideas and look at what libraries are already doing with voice computing.

3

Real-World Uses

Hands-Free Situations

There are many situations where hands-free computing is useful, and this is where digital assistants really shine. Perhaps your hands are dirty, injured, or just busy. One example is during food preparation. With a smart speaker, using your voice, you can make a grocery list, convert units, set multiple timers, control smart appliances, search for recipe ideas (and have them read to you step by step), get cooking times, pair wines with food, and listen to music or news while you're cooking.[1]

Another example is when you are taking care of a baby. Using an Alexa skill called Baby Stats,[2] you can easily track statistics for your baby, like when the baby slept, when the baby was fed, and how much the baby weighs. This is handy for weekly doctor appointments where doctors usually give you a paper form to track these items. Now you can easily speak the items to the app while your hands are busy.[3]

Yet another situation where it would be useful to have a smart speaker is in hospital rooms. If you are bedridden, you could now control the TV, the blinds, and the room temperature, and you could listen to music, all by voice. If you are a patient at home who needs rides to appointments, you could call Lyft or Uber with your smart speaker.[4]

I'm sure you can imagine other situations where getting information with your voice would be useful, such as when you are doing a building project in your workshop or while doing arts and crafts projects.

Workplace Uses

Amazon is working to add Alexa in the workplace. With their new Alexa for Business, companies can build their own skills for internal use, for example, accessing the company calendar or getting information about clients.[5] They are also working to add Alexa to conference rooms, working with Polycom and other video and audio conference providers. Soon you'll be able to control the lights and temperature of workplace conference rooms by voice. There are even efforts to set up recognition of particular voices within a company so that a person can control only the features they have permission to. The WeWork coworking company has been experimenting with these features using their Ask WeWork skill for hearing which meeting rooms are available, extending room reservations, and controlling the lights in meeting rooms.[6]

Integration of Alexa with Microsoft's Office 365 is in the works, with the goal of voice control for scheduling meetings, printing documents, and finding out about your upcoming appointments. Alexa also connects to business software like Salesforce and FinancialForce for voice control of specific tasks.[7]

Another sector using Alexa for Business is the hotel industry. One of the first to do this was Wynn in Las Vegas, where you can use your voice to open curtains, control the TV, turn on the lights, and get news and weather reports.[8] Marriott hotels are testing Alexa and Siri to decide which they will offer. And some Aloft hotels offer Siri-enabled iPads for controlling temperature and lighting and asking concierge questions.[9]

You can learn more about workplace uses on Amazon's Alexa for Business website: https://aws.amazon.com/alexaforbusiness/. To read about ideas for future workplace uses, see "Innovative Uses of Speech Recognition Today," https://www.globalme.net/blog/new-technology-in-speech-recognition.

I'm sure you can imagine how these workplace uses might be useful in your library — for everything from scheduling meetings to looking up a quick fact during a meeting or perhaps accessing your library's usage statistics by voice.

Benefits for the Elderly

Voice computing is turning out to be a boon for the elderly. It's proving useful for both healthy older people and those who need assistance.

A recent study in a community of retirees at Carlsbad by the Sea Retirement Community near San Diego showed that elderly people enjoyed using Alexa and benefited in many ways.[10] The study was conducted by Front Porch Center for Innovation and Wellbeing.[11] They decided to test Alexa because their residents were asking to try it. Their goal was to learn the best ways to integrate smart speakers into its retirement communities across California. Specifically, they wanted to find out if these technologies promoted independence and self-management. They also wanted to assess whether these voice-first devices would help increase social inter-action and engagement levels of adults in their communities.

Most of the people involved in the test were in their late 80s. Some of them used walkers, and some had hearing or visual impair-ments. Some people had hand tremors, making it hard to type or use a smartphone.

The study showed positive results with 100% of respondents say-ing it made their life easier. They used it for tasks like getting weather reports, setting alarms and timers, listening to music and audiobooks, asking for the date and time, listening to news, and searching for information. They also tested smart home features like turning lamps on and adjusting the room temperature. They used the messaging feature of Alexa to call and leave messages between devices with other people in their community.

Further results showed the following:

- Seventy-five percent used their smart devices at least once a day.
- Eighty-two percent reported that using a smart plugged lamp with Alexa was "very easy."

- Ninety-three percent felt their smart home devices increased their overall enjoyment of using the Alexa device.[12]

One of the things that helped make this project a success was that they offered twice monthly workshops called Alexa 101 to answer questions, provide training, and go over the basic features. They provided a printed "cheat sheet" with basic voice commands. They also gave free Pandora accounts to those who had no music streaming service. They upgraded the Wi-Fi bandwidth in their buildings to make sure the deployment would be successful.

To learn more interesting details about this study, read *Amazon "Alexa" Pilot Analysis Report* by Front Porch Center for Innovation and Wellbeing, December 2017, http://fpciw.org/wp-content/uploads/sites/15/2017/12/FINAL-DRAFT-Amazon-Alexa-Analysis-Report.pdf.

Another interesting example of voice computing for the elderly can be found on a blog called *Love My Echo*.[13] One post tells the story of a woman who helps care for her aging mother with poor eyesight who lives across town (still in her own apartment). She loves books but can't read print, so she listens to audiobooks purchased from Audible. Her daughter put the mother's Echo on her own Amazon account, which made it easy to order books that her mother wanted. Her mother could then listen right away to a new book, using voice commands. They also used the shopping list feature together, so the mother could add items by voice and her daughter could pick up those items when shopping. Her mother has trouble dialing or typing on a phone, so she tells Alexa to send a text message that tells her family to call her.

An interesting aspect of all this is that it's easy for the daughter to keep tabs on her mother's well-being without being intrusive. She just looks at the history feature of their shared account to see what her mom is doing. Seeing that she asked for the weather report at 6:30 a.m. made it easy to see that she was up and around for the day. She also noticed when her mom was having trouble sleeping and was talking to Alexa several times during the night.

There are other studies and other commentators discussing successes in this area.[14] I'm sure you can imagine how useful and enjoyable this can be for elderly people you know, and perhaps even think of some library applications. In the next section, we'll discuss some benefits of voice computing for people with disabilities.

Benefits for People with Disabilities

People who are blind or have visual impairments find voice computing very useful. It's also useful for people with mobility issues that
make it hard to move around the house or to type on a keyboard.

Many blind or visually impaired people use screen readers on their
computers or mobile devices. This takes some learning and can be
awkward to use. Now with voice computing, blind users are
enthusiastic about Amazon Echo and similar devices, since they
make life so much easier.

One blogger, Anna Schaverien, writes about her blind father and
the fact that he often asks family members to search Google for
him, because it takes so much time to use a screen reader on his
computer.[15] Now with Alexa, he can get answers right away.
Alexa can't provide the wide variety of answers that a search
engine can, but it's great for the basics, like getting weather reports,
news, sports scores, and listening to music or podcasts. This gives
him more independence, which is a wonderful thing. One annoy-
ing thing about Alexa for the blind, though, is her habit of telling
you to look in the app for more in-depth information for particular
queries. Also, because setting up an Alexa device involves using
the mobile app, it can't be set up only by voice commands.
Luckily Amazon has made the Alexa app for iOS VoiceOver compatible. Luis Pérez, an assistive technology expert with vision
impairments, mentions in his blog post, "Amazon Echo as an
Accessibility Support,"[16] that the app works well for him.

Another interesting way that smart speakers benefit the blind is
through use of Echo Look. As mentioned previously, the Look is an
Alexa product that gives you fashion advice.[17] It uses a built-in camera and LED lighting to take still photos or videos of your outfit for
the day. You activate it by voice, and you can share your photos with
friends or use a companion app to ask Amazon's Style Check service
which outfit looks best on you.[18] Of course, Amazon wants to sell
you clothing, but an interesting use of this is to help blind people
make sure they've chosen clothing that matches and looks good.
Blind user Bill Boules discusses this idea in "Why Amazon's Alexa
Is 'Life Changing' for the Blind."[19] Boules is an associate director of
rehabilitation and reintegration at Vision Center of Excellence. This
is a U.S. Navy office that helps military and their families who are
blind or have vision impairments.

Other features that blind users find helpful are adding calendar appointments, getting reminders, using timers for cooking, ordering meal delivery using the Grubhub skill,[20] ordering grocery deliveries with the Peapod skill,[21] listening to audiobooks, calling Uber or Lyft ride-sharing services by voice, controlling home appliances that lack accessibility features, and controlling other smart home features like thermostats.

Voice Control Helps People with Mobility Impairments

Another group of people who benefit from voice computing are those with mobility impairments. This includes those with quadriplegia, spinal cord injuries, cerebral palsy, multiple sclerosis, amyotrophic lateral sclerosis (ALS), strokes, or brain injuries. When you can't use your hands, but your voice works fine, voice computing is a wonderful solution.

People with these impairments sometimes use a device like Tecla-e, an assistive device that enables the use of smartphones and other computing devices. It connects to switches, joysticks, buttons, and wheelchair driving controls so that people can interact with smartphones, tablets, and computers hands free. This device integrates with Alexa in useful ways. Here's an example:

> If your Amazon Echo is not within earshot and is inaccessible, you can still ask Alexa a command using tecla-e. For example, if you are a quadriplegic and are upstairs in bed, but forgot to turn the lights off downstairs, simply turn on Switch Control on your iPhone or Switch Access on Android, go to the tecla-e companion app, and ask Alexa to turn off your smart lights. The tecla-e companion app is fully accessible using assistive switches saving you the frustration of smart home apps that do not follow universal design principles.[22]

This device works well when syncing it to an Amazon account. It can allow people to control all of their assistive smart devices from one app instead of having to use a variety of apps to control different devices.

What about People with Speech Impairments?

You might be wondering about people with speech impairments. Isn't it difficult or impossible for voice assistants to understand someone with this type of disability? Luckily there are some work-arounds for this. Luis Pérez, an inclusive learning evangelist, talks about using VoiceOver on his iPhone to speak out commands to the Echo.[23] He says that Alexa understood every word. Another solution he recommends is using an AAC[24] app called Proloquo4Text.[25] This app lets you enter frequently used sentences, commands, or questions, and it speaks them out loud for you at the tap of a menu choice. He uses this with his Echo to have it speak commands in a clear voice. You can see a brief demo of this in a YouTube video called "Quick Demo: Using Amazon Echo with Proloquo4Text," https:// youtu.be/bNnuDdmUA9k.

There are newer technologies being developed that help people with speech impairments. A promising mobile app is called Voiceitt, which is designed to understand nonstandard or dysarthric speech.[26] It's a hands-free voice app, and its developers plan to integrate their technology into smart speakers in the future. The app asks you to record useful sentences out loud as a way to train it. It uses machine learning to get more and more familiar with the way you speak. After it's trained, the app can turn your statements into normalized speech, with output as text or audio. You can watch a short video demo on the Voiceitt website: http:// www.voiceitt.com/why-voiceitt.html. This also shows promise for people with different accents.

Given all of these uses, it's no wonder that people with disabilities are enthusiastic about voice computing. Since librarians are dedicated to providing access to all, it's time that we consider smart speakers or other voice assistants for inclusion in our accessibility workstations or conference rooms. We can also provide information about these devices to our users with disabilities. More ideas for this are provided in the next section.

Use in Libraries

You may be wondering how you might integrate voice computing into your library services, given all the emphasis on home use and also because voice computing tends to be used in places where you have the privacy to speak out loud.

But there *are* libraries experimenting with this technology and writing interesting articles about what it means for our future. In the next few sections, you'll take a look at some specific examples from school libraries, public libraries, and academic libraries. You'll also look at what universities and their students are doing to create skills for Amazon Alexa and how library vendors are beginning to consider integrating voice computing into their products. It's a good time to get up to date on this technology while it's still young, since experts are predicting that voice computing will develop quickly and be an important trend in the coming years.[27]

School Libraries

In 2015, only a few months after Amazon Echo was released, school librarian Gwyneth Jones set an Echo up in her library and blogged about it.[28] She invited kids to ask Alexa questions when they came into the library. She wrote about what students were using it for—tasks such as getting the title of a book, spelling and defining words, telling the time, getting weather forecasts, playing music, and listening to audiobooks.

She noted that it was most interesting to watch the students learn how to phrase questions so Alexa could more easily answer them. You can watch a couple of short videos in her blog post to see her students and their reactions.[29]

Another school library media specialist, Sarah FitzHenry, of Charlottesville, Virginia, blogged about her experience with Google Home in her school library.[30] She focused on grades three through eight and did presentations for her school about Google Home, how it works, her library's policies for it, and best ways to use it.[31] She created a new Google account just for their smart speaker. This account is not linked to any personal information or calendars, and there are no names in the address book. This prevents students from accidentally sending messages with it.

She pointed out that it's easy to keep tabs on how students are using it, since you can access a list of all the queries (with audio recordings) in the history of the Google Assistant app. She created presentations and signage to make students aware of the rules and policies, and kids know there are consequences if they don't follow the rules.

When parents and teachers asked her about the safety of Google Home, she gave this response:

I get this question a lot, from parents, students, and teachers. I've done a lot of research on the subject and have found one answer again and again—Google Home is safe if we decide to use it safely. It's up to us to use internet safety rules, act as good Digital Citizens, and behave safely when we use this new tool. We cover this in depth in my introductory presentation. The truth is that most students already have these tools in their pockets in the form of Siri, or on their laptops—this is just a new opportunity to teach them to use it safely. Google Home has inspired some great conversations about internet safety and privacy that we might not have had otherwise. I'm grateful to have this example to work with to better teach students about how to stay safe online.[32]

Students know that they are supposed to use Google Home one person at a time, except during certain games. She turns the microphone off during library classes, and students know to come back later when classes are happening. She hasn't needed to use the school's information technology (IT) department to manage it, since it's so easy to set up and maintain.

To see a video of her students using it, read her excellent blog post, "Google Home in the School Library: FAQ."[33] Students ask Google about authors, book series, book titles, and general information. Her post is inspiring because she has addressed everyone's concerns so well and prepped her community thoroughly for the use of this new technology. She also uses it as a way to teach students about good digital citizenship.

School Classrooms

Many classroom teachers are writing about using Alexa or Google Home in classrooms. They give tips for practical use, such as putting it in an area that every student can reach, allowing only one student at a time to use it, and keeping a notebook of questions and phrases that work well.[34] Some ideas for lessons include seeing if students can use a calculator more quickly than Alexa to do math calculations, asking for synonyms during writing workshops, and linking Alexa to a Google Calendar used for classroom events and field trips so they can query it by voice.[35]

To see lesson plans, handouts, and other creative ideas for classroom use, search the site Teachers Pay Teachers, where K–12 teachers share and sell lesson plans: https://www.teacherspayteachers.com. Search for "ask Alexa," or "Amazon Echo," to find activities and handouts.

Another interesting example is found in a podcast episode from *The 10-Minute Teacher Show with Vicki Davis*. In episode 108, "Amazon Echo in the Classroom," she interviews teacher Bill Selak.[36] In his school he found that first- and second-grade classrooms were the sweet spot where the kind of learning available with Alexa made the most sense.

Here is a quote from the podcast transcript where students learned about what kinds of questions a database can answer:

> So I love just the inquiry that second-graders do around it. When they got it, it was just, what questions do you have. . . . And they went through, like, what's a question that a database can answer and can't answer, and talked about opinions and facts. And it led into so many amazing authentic discussions.
>
> Instead of just saying, today, we're talking about fact and opinion; you can frame it around, so Alexa didn't answer this question because it's an opinion, let's talk about that. So it became just really authentic learning that was much more student-driven than it otherwise would have been.[37]

For more interesting examples of classroom use, see "Alexa, Can We Go to School Today?"[38] and "Alexa, How Can You Improve Teaching and Learning?"[39] Since teachers are using this in classrooms, it's a good idea for librarians to be familiar with it as well and to experiment with smart speakers of different platforms.

Public Libraries

Public libraries are experimenting with smart speakers in some interesting ways. Some are loaning out Amazon Echo or Google Home. Others are offering workshops on how to use them effectively. And some are offering Alexa skills for finding out about library news and events. In addition, some library vendors are experimenting with integrating their products and services with voice computing. Let's look at a few examples.

Loaning Smart Speakers The Framingham Public Library in Massachusetts offers a few Amazon Echos and Google Homes for their users to borrow.[40] They remind people that they will need an Android or iOS device to set them up, a home Wi-Fi network, an Amazon or Google account, and the mobile app for each device. They loan each device for 14 days with no renewals. They instruct users to reset the device to its factory settings before returning it. You can see their circulation policies here: https://framinghamlibrary. org/amazon-echo and https://framinghamlibrary.org/google-home. It's interesting to see libraries treating these devices in a similar way as tablets or e-readers that circulate.

Using Smart Speakers in the Library   The Missouri Valley Public Library in Iowa has an Amazon Echo that people can use in the library.[41] They keep the Echo by the front desk and invite people who come into the library to ask questions. You might consider placing a smart speaker in a quiet conference room. Perhaps it could be marketed as part of an accessibility workstation, since users with visual impairments find these so useful.

Library Instruction   Some libraries are offering events where the public can learn about voice computing. The Grande Prairie Public Library in Illinois held an event for general audiences called Amazon's Alexa.[42] The Tuscarawas County Public Library System in Ohio had an event aimed at seniors, called Never Too Late to Learn: Tech for Seniors—Google Home vs. Amazon Echo.[43] The Westport Library in Connecticut offered an event for learning how to create skills for Alexa; see "Amazon Alexa Voice Services Bootcamp."[44]

In addition to these ideas, consider including instruction about voice computing into any of your technology classes, one-on-one technology assistance, and in sessions about security and privacy online.

Alexa Skills for Libraries   If you search Amazon's Alexa Skills store, you'll find a few skills that use information from public libraries. These are not written by the libraries themselves but are unofficial skills written by third-party developers using open application programming interfaces (APIs). Here are some examples.

Library News and Hot Fiction   There are two skills from the Los Angeles Public Library, one is a flash briefing skill with news from their blog and the other is their list of hot fiction.[45] These don't appear to be official skills from the library itself; the developer is listed as "Rampaging Robot." But they work and are likely using freely available information, such as the RSS feed from the library's blog.

Search the Catalog   A skill called Houston Library lets you search the Houston Public Library by voice.[46] This one is also not by the library itself but by an independent developer. Likewise, a similar skill is called Toronto Library Unofficial.[47]

Some library catalog vendors are planning to offer this kind of integration at some point, with more features, such as placing items on hold and hearing what titles you have out.

Library Events   Some libraries are creating skills for learning about events in the library. One skill is from the Worthington Libraries, Ohio Library, called Worthington Libraries.[48] Here are some sample questions you can ask: "What's happening today at Worthington Park Library?" "Are there any events for teens this weekend at Northwest Library?" "What's going on tomorrow at Old Worthington Library?" For more information about events, say "get details." You can navigate through event details by saying "next," "previous," or "repeat."[49]

Another skill for voice-controlled news about library events is available through a service called Burbio.[50] It's a service where local community groups (including libraries) can list their calendars. Users of Burbio (accounts are free) can then subscribe to multiple calendars from their local schools, libraries, and community groups, easily consolidating all the information into their own calendars. Burbio provides mobile apps for Android and iOS and also an Alexa skill.[51] The Pompton Lakes Library in New Jersey offers this skill to their patrons so they can ask Alexa about upcoming library events.[52] You can learn more about the Burbio skill for Alexa, and see a video demo here: http://alexa.burbio.com/alexa.

Academic Libraries

Loaning Smart Speakers   Like public libraries, some academic libraries are loaning out smart speakers. For example, Vogel Library at Wartburg College in Waverly, Iowa, loans out an Echo Dot as part of their technology equipment loans.[53] They loan it for up to four hours while the library is open. They handle it the same way as they do other equipment like calculators, headphones, chargers, cables, adapters, and speakers. Many college libraries loan out similar equipment, and it's not difficult to add smart speakers to the list.

Skills from University Libraries   It doesn't appear that many academic libraries are creating skills yet, but a few have. One example is from the Iowa State University Library. Their skill is called IowaStateLibFacts.[54] With this skill, you can ask for facts about library collections, art, library spaces, and library history. The library at California State University, San Bernardino, has partnered with their IT department to include their news in a skill called CSUSB News.[55] You can ask for news from Strategic Communication, Athletics, The Technology Support Center, and John M. Pfau Library.

In the early days of mobile app development, only a few libraries had mobile apps or mobile-friendly websites, but today it's a different story. No doubt we'll see more libraries creating skills in the future.

Skills from Universities   Many universities now have skills in the Alexa store. Some are created by third parties (perhaps students) and some by the university departments themselves. A few skills by universities are MIT Facts, Lehigh University, The Ohio State Skill, University of San Diego, OU Facts, and OU Directory (University of Oklahoma).[56] These skills offer random facts about the university, and some give schedules of upcoming events, directory searches of phone numbers and emails, hours of campus locations, and sports records.

University Students Are Developing Alexa Skills   Amazon has been working with students and universities to encourage students to learn to create skills and design voice interfaces. One of the first programs to do this was at Arizona State University (ASU), beginning in the fall of 2017.[57] This program was for engineering students in a new residence hall. They could choose to get a free Echo Dot and then sign up for courses about building voice interfaces with Alexa. Sixteen hundred Dot speakers were donated by Amazon for this program.[58] Along with this effort, ASU created a skill for getting information about the campus and campus events.[59]

Another university that is promoting this learning is University of Oklahoma. They provided about 600 Echo Dots to students on their campus. They suggested skills for students to try, and they held a hackathon where students developed Alexa skills.[60]

Amazon has set up Amazon Alexa Fund Fellowship, which includes four universities: Carnegie Mellon University, University of Waterloo, University of Southern California, and Johns Hopkins University. This is a year-long program that offers students funding, mentoring, and access to Alexa devices. The purpose is to develop an undergraduate or graduate curriculum around the disciplines of text-to-speech, natural language understanding, automatic speech recognition, and conversational artificial intelligence.[61]

Amazon has also set up Alexa Prize, with the first winners being student developers from University of Washington.[62] As mentioned in Chapter 2 in the section "Is It Possible to Monetize a Skill?" winners received a research grant of $250,000.[63]

With all this emphasis on students learning to develop skills and design voice interfaces, it will be increasingly important for academic libraries to be familiar with the basics of voice computing and to offer resources to support it.

It's Still the Early Days of Voice Computing   This is still the early days of voice computing. It sometimes feels similar to the early days of mobile apps and smartphones. A few libraries are experimenting with voice computing, and some library vendors are beginning to implement voice computing or discuss implementing it. As with any emerging technology, it's a good idea to set up small experiments and get feedback from library users.[64] Because voice computing is so promising for people with disabilities, it's important for librarians to become familiar with these technologies. We should consider how we can use voice computing to help provide access to all for many sorts of information resources. As with any new technology, there are privacy concerns to be aware of. The next chapter focuses on the privacy and ethical concerns of voice computing.

4

Privacy and Ethical Concerns

The Privacy of Your Voice Data

Many people feel wary about voice computing because the idea of having a microphone listening to you in your private home feels intrusive. It's easy to imagine nightmare scenarios with that kind of access to your conversations.

How to Control Your Voice Data

Luckily, there are ways to control and make private your voice data. The first thing to know is that even though smart speakers need to be listening for the wake word in order to function, they don't record anything until you speak your question. They stop when the device speaks its answer. *The recordings consist of the questions you ask and nothing more.*

Another thing that's good to know is that with Amazon Alexa and Google Home, you can go into the associated app or website to delete your recordings—one by one or all of your voice history.[1] Amazon and Google use this information to improve the intelligence of their systems, so they give you a warning when you begin to delete your recordings. But these devices work fine when you first get them, without any of your history, so if you want to delete your history, there is no reason not to. Apple handles this a bit differently for Siri on HomePod. They anonymize your voice data so it's not connected to your identity. And they delete their collected, anonymized data (which they use to train Siri) every six months.[2]

In addition to deleting your recordings, you can turn off the microphone on your smart speaker. Amazon Echo has a button on the top. When you push it, the ring turns red to show that the microphone is off.[3] Google Home has a button in the back, and after you press it, the indicator light will turn orange, and it will respond by voice to tell you the microphone is off.[4] On Apple's HomePod, you can say, "Hey Siri, stop listening," or you can use the Home app on your iPhone to turn off the microphone.[5] So with all of these smart speakers, you can turn off the microphone when you're not planning on using it. This is handy when you're listening to a TV show or podcast about smart speakers. This can keep your speaker from trying to respond when someone on the show says the wake word.

Block Incoming Voice Calls

Another privacy concern might be that one of your contacts could listen to conversations in your room when they call you on the speaker. Amazon calls this Drop In. You can set up particular contacts to be able to "drop in" and have a voice conversation from their Echo to yours. You can block all calls by turning on "do not disturb" mode in the app. In the Alexa app, you can also turn off Drop In entirely, block specific people, or set it to "household only" for using multiple devices in your house as an intercom system.[6] With Google Home, you can connect your personal phone number so you can be called from a Google Home. You don't need to enable this, but if you already have, you can turn it off in the app.[7]

Disable Voice Purchases

If you worry about people in your home purchasing items from Amazon by voice and charging them to your account, you'll be happy to know that it's easy to turn off voice purchasing. Just turn it off in the Alexa app. If you like to purchase by voice sometimes, you can add a voice code that you set in the app so someone needs to know the code to purchase. Since it's easy for your children to overhear you, another option is to set up Alexa to recognize the voices of different people in your household and only allow certain voices to make purchases.[8]

Privacy Recommendations for Design of Voice Interfaces

The American Civil Liberties Union (ACLU) has written a privacy guidelines document for developers of voice-computing systems. Here are a few examples from it:

- "Users should have access to any of their audio recordings that a company retains, and the option to delete them."
- "Speech fragments transmitted to companies should be retained for the minimal necessary period, should not be shared absent a warrant, and should not be used for other purposes."
- "It should also become standard to build in a hardware power switch that physically cuts off electricity to a microphone so that consumers can stop a microphone from recording."
- "Special attention should be paid to any capability for remote activation of recording. Best for privacy is for no such activation to be possible."[9]

Luckily Apple, Amazon, and Google already comply with these guidelines.

Children and Voice Assistants

You might wonder about the privacy issues involved in voice computing for children. Under Children's Online Privacy Protection Act (COPPA), it is illegal to collect the voice recordings of children under age 13, without parental consent. However, in the fall of 2017, the Federal Trade Commission (FTC) advised companies that they would not enforce the law (which began in 1999), as long as recordings of children's voices were only used to transcribe commands and not stored for other uses.[10] They did this in recognition that voice can be a replacement for typing. One exception to this is asking for a child's name in a skill. This requires parental consent, since it's in the category of "personal data."[11]

Amazon handles these issues by asking for parental permission the first time you enable a skill aimed at children. You are asked to verify either by a text message sent to your phone or by credit card on Amazon's site.[12] Once you do this, you can enable as many skills for children as you like without further verification. Google handles this in a similar way.[13] Their "apps for families" program requires parental permission to activate. It's also possible to set up Google accounts for children under age 13 powered by Family Link.[14] Using this, parents can manage their children's Google accounts and limit what they can do. Both platforms offer a way to train your smart speaker to recognize different people's voices in your household. Google's Tips for Families gives tips for parents on how to protect the privacy of your children.[15]

In the spring of 2018, Amazon came out with Echo Dot Kids Edition.[16] As mentioned in Chapter 2, this version of the Dot comes with Amazon FreeTime on Alexa, an Alexa service built with kids in mind. It includes a dashboard of parental controls for filtering content and controlling the times it can be used. It also includes a one-year free trial of FreeTime Unlimited for access to more educational content, so you can see that Amazon is considering use by children with these offerings.

Ethical Concerns about Children and Voice Computing

Many parents like voice computing with smart speakers because it can be a family or group activity. It keeps kids from being glued to the screens of their phones or tablets, and it's also easy for parents to see a child's history of voice interactions in the mobile app.[17] Games on smart speakers encourage you to interact with the people around you instead of being solitary. A recent study published by tech consultancy Accenture showed that two-thirds of respondents used their smartphones less when they had a smart speaker.[18]

That said, some worry about kids becoming bossy if they can order their smart assistant around or lazy because it's so easy to do things by voice. These issues are explored in an article called "Growing Up with Alexa," by Rachel Metz in *MIT Technology Review*.[19] She spoke to several experts, including Kaveri Subrahmanyam, a developmental psychologist and chair of child and family studies at California State University, Los Angeles. She and other experts were generally optimistic, seeing this new way of interacting as less distracting, more social, and useful in helping small children build social skills. Some pointed out that with services like Twitter, it's easier to behave in harassing ways since you feel somewhat hidden by the abstraction of the service. Voice computing feels more like face-to-face conversations and therefore encourages more empathy in interactions.

An interesting study was done in 2017 at the MIT Media Lab, called " 'Hey Google Is It OK If I Eat You?': Initial Explorations in Child-Agent Interaction."[20] In this study researchers found that sometimes kids engaged with voice assistants as peers and other times as teachers. Kids believed that they could both learn from their digital assistants and also teach them. The study concluded that perhaps in the future, we could design voice computing so that kids are able to tinker with and program the agents "and thus expand their perception of their own intelligence and different ways to develop it."[21] This has already started to come true with the release of the app Be a Maker, discussed in Chapter 2—it's designed for kids ages 7–12 and makes it easy for them to program behavior of a voice-controlled home robot called Jibo.[22]

Recognizing the Speech of Young Children

Another issue when it comes to children and voice computing is whether these devices can recognize young children's speech. One company working to solve this is Soapbox Labs.[23] They have created an application programming interface (API) for developers to use in things like voice-controlled toys and Alexa skills. It's designed to recognize the speech of children between 4 and 12 years old. It can handle the fact that kids sometimes shout or pronounce things in unusual ways. It has been trained with speech data from children, unlike Alexa and Google Assistant, which have been trained with the speech of adults. They hope to make this technology available not only for developers of toys and games but also for educational content like voice-controlled reading and language tutors.[24]

Voice Computing for Children Is Here to Stay

In spite of all the possible dangers, when it comes to children and voice computing, the technology is here and is being used by many people and organizations. It seems likely that it will only become more common in classrooms and homes, so the best course of action is to continue to advocate for strong privacy protections and for ethical use of this technology. This is another reason why it's important for librarians to understand these issues—school, public, and academic libraries have young users already familiar with voice computing, and we need to understand and plan for the best use cases in library services.

Sexism in Voice Computing

Another ethical issue that comes up with voice computing is sexism. Have you wondered why most voice assistants use female voices? Amazon tested many voices in their internal beta program before launching and found that people preferred female voices.[25] Alexa offers only a female voice. Siri and Google Assistant have the option to switch to a male voice, but a female voice is the default. Some say that female voices are easier to understand, but this has been debunked by research.[26] There are, however, studies that show people prefer women's voices over men's, saying that it's because female voices are warmer.[27]

A digital assistant can be like your private secretary, someone who is efficient and reliable but not in charge. Other artificial intelligence (AI) voices, like IBM's Watson, which won Jeopardy, and works with physicians on cancer treatments, have male voices. According to research, people prefer masculine-sounding voices from leaders.[28] In the book *Wired for Speech: How Voice Activates and Advances the Human-Computer Relationship*, Stanford University professor Clifford Nass noted that people perceive female voices as helpers for solving our problems and male voices as authority figures who tell us what to do.[29]

Because of all this, it's easy to see that we are replicating our current cultural norms in these technologies. Some are questioning this: Are we reinforcing harmful stereotypes about gender roles? What effect will this have on society? It's worth considering.[30]

Beyond reinforcing the idea of women as subservient and passive, there is the issue of people speaking sexually harassing phrases to voice assistants (even if jokingly). In early 2017, a team from the news outlet Quartz created a test to compare the responses of Alexa, Google, Siri, and Cortana to harassing and insulting phrases. They found many examples of responses that were passive, accepting, and even flirty.[31] For example, when Siri was told she was a slut, she responded, "I'd blush if I could."

This led to the filing of a petition by *Care2.com*, which called on Apple and Amazon to reprogram their digital assistants to give more assertive responses to these types of questions.[32] By the time it was filed, Amazon had already heard from customers and gave Alexa a "disengage mode." By that they meant that she responds in ways that disengage from the conversation. Her responses to harassing questions include "I'm not going to respond to that" and "I'm not sure what outcome you expected."[33] In addition, when you ask Alexa if she's a feminist, she says yes. She adds, "As is anyone who believes in bridging the inequality between men and women in society."[34]

It's great that people are asking the developers of these technologies to be aware of issues like these and make changes. I hope we will keep pushing for awareness of ethical issues and petitioning companies like Apple, Amazon, and Google to make changes that reflect this awareness.

What Librarians Need to Know

As with all new technologies, there are many fears about what these new tools will mean for society. News headlines tend to stress fear and negativity, since that sells advertising.[35] Sometimes you may feel so overwhelmed about privacy issues that you end up not using and therefore not benefiting from useful new technologies.[36]

When you understand how these tools work, you can make informed decisions and take a balanced view of the privacy issues. You can use these tools in smart ways for yourself and also help others use them effectively.

Here is a quick checklist of the top tips for protecting privacy with smart speakers:

- Recordings are only captured from the time you say the wake word until the speaker responds. These are encrypted while they travel from the device to Amazon or Google's servers.
- You can turn the microphone off anytime on smart speakers from Amazon, Google, and Apple.
- You can delete the history of your voice recordings from Amazon and Google. Apple doesn't match the recordings to

your identity but instead anonymizes them. They delete them every six months.

- You can disable voice purchasing from Amazon and Google. This is important to do on a smart speaker being used by the public in your library.
- If you want to use voice purchasing, you can set up voice recognition with Amazon and Google so that only recognized voices can purchase items (you train it in advance). You can also set a PIN code for voice purchasing.
- It's a good idea to use two-factor authentication on your Amazon and Google accounts in order to decrease the likelihood of your accounts being hacked (it's not likely but is possible) and someone reading the transcripts of the questions you asked.[37]
- You can always set up a new account with Amazon or Google for use with your smart speaker. This is useful for a device to be used by the public in your library, since it wouldn't connect to anyone's calendars or address book.
- You should only allow "drop-in" calls on Amazon Echo with close friends and family members, since they can drop in and listen to what's happening in your room. You may want to limit this to use as an intercom within your own house.

Keeping these features in mind will help you use voice computing effectively and safely.

5

The Future of Voice Computing

A Primary Way of Using Computers

As mentioned in Chapter 1, people are quickly adopting smart speakers, even more quickly than during the early days of smartphones.[1] Gartner Research predicts that "by 2020, 30 percent of web browsing sessions will be done without a screen" because of voice-first computing.[2] Several other experts predict that by 2020, more than 200 billion searches will be by voice. And in four years, fewer than 5% of computing devices will have keyboards.[3]

More than one expert predicts that voice will become a primary way of using computers and that it's the future of search and online commerce.[4] They don't see it as replacing typing—just supplementing it in those situations where it makes sense.

Some analysts say that voice will be everywhere, in all kinds of devices.[5] Currently there are many different devices from different manufacturers, with different wake words and apps to manage them. Some vendors are hoping for a future where a smart hub system manages everything in your home so you can control your appliances, speakers, lights, or anything by speaking in a straightforward way, using one wake word for the whole house.[6]

User experience expert Adam Babajee-Pycroft makes the case that Alexa is more important than iPhone in how it will impact society.[7] That's because voice is so intuitive—you don't need to learn a user interface. And because it's more natural to talk than to look down into a screen, it can help us move away from smartphone addiction, with the interruptions it creates in people's daily lives. Another interesting advantage is that we will no longer have to wait a couple of years for an update to a new phone to get new features. Instead, features will be powered by services that live in the cloud and can be updated daily. Developers will add new features without people needing to upgrade their hardware.

Artificial intelligence (AI) expert Gaurav Sharma predicts that as of 2015, we are entering a new era of intelligent assistants.[8] This is due to advances in natural language processing, machine learning, and voice recognition. He paints this as a 10-year paradigm change: 1995 began the web era, 2005 began the mobile app era, and 2015 began the era of intelligent assistants (with the release of Amazon Echo). He and others call this the cognitive computing era. This is computing that emulates strengths of the human brain, including understanding natural language and putting big data into context. It's based on systems that use machine learning to perform tasks in an intelligent way.[9] This era follows the era of programmatic computing, which allowed the creation of data by processing numbers—now we make sense of data, using adaptive, interactive systems.

Technology journalist Antonio García Martinez has an interesting take on this future:

> Between touchscreens and voice, most people in the future won't even know how to touch-type, and typing will go back to being a specialist practitioner's skill, limited to long-form authors, programmers, and (perhaps) antiquarian hipsters who also own fixies and roast their own coffee. My 2-year-old daughter will likely never learn how to drive (and every pedal-to-the-metal, "flooring it" driving analogy will be lost on her), instead issuing voice commands to her self-driving car. And she'll also not know what QWERTY is, or have her left pinkie wired to the mental notion of the letter "Q," as I do so subconsciously I reach for it without even thinking. Instead, she'll speak into an empty room and expect the global hive-mind, along with its AI handmaidens, to answer.[10]

And finally, according to Sundar Pichai, the CEO of Google: "Looking to the future, the next big step will be for the very concept of the 'device' to fade away. Over time, the computer itself—whatever its form factor—will be an intelligent assistant helping you through your day. We will move from mobile first to an AI first world."[11]

All of this is possible because of recent advances in the underlying technologies: natural language processing, speech recognition, and machine learning. This is what we'll look at in the next section.

Advances in Speech Recognition and Natural Language Processing

Voice technologies such as speech recognition and natural language processing have improved substantially in recent years. Microsoft has announced breakthroughs in AI that allow its automated speech transcription to surpass human error levels.[12] In May 2018, Google announced a new technology for automating phone calls in ways that sound completely human, making it possible for humans to speak normally with it, as they would to a person. It's called Google Duplex and uses deep neural networks to make robocalls sound like real humans.[13]

Automatic Speech Recognition (ASR) is the ability for computers to recognize spoken words. This technology progressed slowly until 2010, when accuracy levels improved dramatically. Between 2010 and 2015, this accuracy improved beyond all the advancements in the previous 40 years.[14] As of 2017, word error rates were under 7% according to an article in *IEEE Spectrum*.[15] This was attributed to the convergence of several technologies that have improved dramatically: AI, processing power, mobile devices, and more.

One of the reasons these technologies have improved so much is that the massive data centers operated by Google and Amazon are constantly learning from conversations happening around the world. Whenever someone speaks to their device, no matter what the language or the accent, Google and Amazon learn more about how people talk. Other companies working on AI that can understand speech and respond intelligently are IBM, China's Baidu, and several start-ups. It's expected that this will keep improving and that computers may end up understanding speech better than humans do.[16]

One of the problems that is still an issue is the ability to have real conversations, with back-and-forth interactions that understand context. This is a very difficult problem, as you can imagine. People tend to speak in halting ways, repeat themselves, stumble over words, and so on. We tend to interrupt during the middle of an answer. One advance that shows promise is from Microsoft. They have announced "full duplexing," the ability to have a conversation with a digital assistant where it can speak and listen simultaneously.[17] This makes it possible for a human to interrupt during a response and ask for something else.

A start-up from Cambridge, Massachusetts, called Gamalon, is working on a new technique for teaching computers to handle language. It offers a way to deal with multiple meanings, with the computer making smart judgments about phrases that are ambiguous. It also offers a memory of what's being discussed, so you can ask follow-up questions like "What about tomorrow?" after asking for today's weather.[18]

Another issue still being worked on is background noise. This can make it hard for devices to understand speech. They don't easily distinguish between the sounds of a dog barking or a plane overhead and spoken words. So far, engineers need to collect sounds like those and program devices to filter them out. But over time, experts predict that as we add more data to these large systems, this will make speech recognition more and more accurate.[19] These improvements will eventually help improve noise suppression, far-field voice interaction, and multispeaker interaction (devices talking to each other).[20]

With the dramatic increase in numbers of people using Alexa, Amazon has access to a gigantic repository of speech interactions. This gives them an edge over Google, which has long had an edge because of its database of text search queries. A look at Amazon's job listings shows that they have thousands of people working on these challenges. There are usually over 1,000 jobs related to Alexa, spread over a dozen departments around the world, as well as over 100 openings for machine-learning specialists.[21] In addition to the challenges of understanding human speech, they are working on improving the sound of Alexa's voice for more natural sounding conversation. They use machine learning to train the synthetic voice, using a database of human narrators. It's helpful that they own the Audible audiobook publisher, which contains many recordings of professional narrations.[22]

We still have a long way to go for computers to hold a realistic, longer conversation with people. This would involve judging the human's intent. For example, humans can usually infer that if their friends say they haven't been to the gym in weeks, they really want to talk about stress or body image. For software, that's very difficult to do. But for the kinds of tasks we are asking of our voice assistants, the future looks promising, with many improvements making these tools more useful than they currently are.

Possible Uses in Libraries

I hope that after reading this guide, you can more easily imagine some ways that voice computing could be used in library services. We are still in the early stages of this new technology, and what seems basic now will likely seem primitive in 5 or 10 years. If the predictions of experts are correct, and this truly is the beginning of a whole new era of computing, then it's certainly worth learning about, experimenting with, and considering how voice computing can be used thoughtfully and effectively in libraries.[23]

The next time you are working on a building project for a new library, or renovating your current building, you may have options to choose to include voice computing in conference or meeting rooms. As discussed in Chapter 3, you might use voice computing to schedule meetings, initiate conference calls, ask for basic information, and control lights and temperature of the room.

When it comes to meeting the needs of our users with various disabilities, voice computing shows promise for people with vision or mobility impairments. We could add smart speakers to accessibility workstations in private rooms so users can speak out loud without disturbing others. Even though the information you can get from Alexa, Siri, or Google Assistant is very basic right now, it's likely to improve in the future as a way to search more in-depth content, such as that from library databases.

Since some library vendors (Demco, OverDrive, EBSCO, and Library Thing) are beginning to consider offering voice search in some of their products, we need to be up to date and aware of various options so we can negotiate effectively for the best design for our users.[24] We also need to understand the privacy implications so we can advocate for protecting people's privacy.[25]

As forward-thinking librarians have always done, we need to experiment with emerging technologies in order to understand them and find out how they might best serve our users.[26] When you market voice-computing services as experimental, you can collect feedback from your users about what worked and what could be improved—through usability tests, surveys, and focus groups. This kind of experimentation will give you realistic data to inform your future decisions, before spending a lot of money on something that may not pan out. Luckily, the cost of a smart speaker is relatively low, so it's not expensive to get started with this technology.

Another good reason to experiment now is that when a technology is still in the early stages, you have the chance to influence future development. You saw an example of this in Chapter 4 where advocates petitioned Amazon and Apple to change responses of Alexa and Siri to sexually harassing language.[27]

If you've worked in libraries for any length of time, you've likely experienced that user expectations for some services can be higher than what we have the ability to provide, given technological and financial limitations. But of course, the forward-thinking among us would like to try, and we often succeed in moving libraries into the future, meeting user needs in innovative and creative ways. I hope this short book has inspired you to experiment and move forward with voice-computing technologies in ways that will delight your users and go beyond their expectations.

Notes

Chapter 1

1. Bret Kinsella, "New Voicebot Report Says Nearly 20% of U.S. Adults Have Smart Speakers," *Voicebot.ai*, March 7, 2018, https://www.voicebot.ai/2018/03/07/new-voicebot-report-says-nearly-20-u-s-adults-smart-speakers/.

2. Sarah Perez, "47.3 Million U.S. Adults Have Access to a Smart Speaker, Report Says," TechCrunch, March 7, 2018, https://techcrunch.com/2018/03/07/47-3-million-u-s-adults-have-access-to-a-smart-speaker-report-says/.

3. See George Anders, "Alexa, Understand Me," *MIT Technology Review*, August 9, 2017, https://www.technologyreview.com/s/608571/alexa-understand-me/; Gaurav Sharma, "The Rise of Intelligent 'Voice' Assistants (I.A.)," *Chatbots Magazine*, May 29, 2016, https://chatbotsmagazine.com/intelligent-assistants-i-a-85c21f9d3b8e.

4. Roger Gorman, "What Does Alexa for Business Really Mean for Our Workplaces?" ITProPortal, January 12, 2018, https://www.itproportal.com/features/what-does-alexa-for-business-really-mean-for-our-workplaces/; James A. Martin, "7 Things Businesses Should Know about Alexa in the Workplace," *CMSWire*, February 6, 2018, https://www.cmswire.com/digital-workplace/7-things-businesses-should-know-about-alexa-in-the-workplace/.

5. Elizabeth Woyke, "The Octogenarians Who Love Amazon's Alexa," *MIT Technology Review*, June 9, 2017, https://www.technologyreview.com/s/608047/the-octogenarians-who-love-amazons-alexa/; "How Does the Amazon Echo Help People with a Vision Impairment?" RNIB, April 6, 2017, http://www.rnib.org.uk/nb-online/how-does-amazon-echo-help-disabled-people.

6. See the web page for an Amazon Echo that circulates at the Framingham Public Library, accessed May 15, 2018, https://framinghamlibrary.org/amazon-echo, and the event listing for a workshop for seniors at a public library: "Never Too Late to Learn: Tech for Seniors—Google Home vs. Amazon Echo—Main" at Tuscarawas Public Library System, accessed May 15, 2018, https://www.tusclibrary.org/content/never-too-late-learn-tech-seniors-google-home-vs-amazon-echo-main.

7. "What Is a Chatbot?" Happiest Minds, the Mindful IT Company, accessed May 15, 2018, https://www.happiestminds.com/Insights/chatbots/.

8. "The 2017 Voice Report Executive Summary," Alpine.AI, January 15, 2017, https://alpine.ai/the-2017-voice-report-by-alpine/. Download the report here: https://s3-us-west-1.amazonaws.com/voicelabs/report/vl-voice-report-exec-summary _final.pdf.

9. Accessed May 15, 2018, http://whatis.techtarget.com/definition/voice -assistant.

10. This is not viewable unless you sign up to be a developer, but you can read quotes from it here: Kim Wetzel, "What Is Alexa? It's Amazon's Virtual Voice Assistant," Digital Trends, May 11, 2018, https://www.digitaltrends.com/home/ what-is-amazons-alexa-and-what-can-it-do/.

11. Jon Reed, "How to Use Amazon Alexa Devices as Bluetooth Speakers for Your iPhone," iPhoneFAQ, June 25, 2017, https://www.iphonefaq.org/archives/ 976036.

12. There is also an open-source voice platform called Mycroft: https:// mycroft.ai/. It was created by a start-up in Kansas City, Missouri, and began as a Kickstarter project. You need to be familiar with command lines and GitHub to set it up, so it's not for the average consumer. Learn more in Jared Newman', "Can Mycroft's Privacy-Centric Voice Assistant Take on Alexa and Google?" *Fast Company*, January 29, 2018, https://www.fastcompany .com/40522226/can-mycrofts-privacy-centric-voice-assistant-take-on-alexa-and -google.

13. See a complete list of Alexa devices on Amazon's site, accessed May 15, 2018, https://www.amazon.com/Amazon-Echo-And-Alexa-Devices/b?ie=UTF8& node=9818047011, and see the Sonos product on Sonos site, accessed May 15, 2018, https://www.sonos.com/en-us/shop/one.html.

14. See a complete list of devices on Google's site, accessed May 15, 2018, https://store.google.com/product/google_home.

15. "Lenovo Smart Display with Google Assistant," https://www.lenovo.com/ us/en/smart-display/, accessed July 26, 2018. Learn about other devices with Google Assistant in Kellen, "Here Are the Google Assistant Speakers with Smart Displays," Droid Life, January 9, 2018, https://www.droid-life.com/2018/01/09/ google-assistant-speakers-smart-displays/.

16. Learn more about HomePod on Apple's site, accessed May 15, 2018, https://www.apple.com/homepod/.

17. Learn more about Cortana on Microsoft's site, accessed May 15, 2018, https://www.microsoft.com/en-us/cortana, and more about the Invoke, accessed May 15, 2018, https://www.microsoft.com/en-us/store/d/harman-kardon -invoke-with-cortana-by-microsoft/8rl7xlnwn95v?activetab=pivot%3aoverviewtab.

18. Such as the Eufy Genie Smart Speaker, accessed May 15, 2018, https:// www.amazon.com/gp/product/B071JN3KYN/.

19. Siri is on certain models of Apple TV, using the remote. "Use Siri on Your Apple TV 4K or Apple TV (4th Generation)," Apple, accessed May 15, 2018, https://support.apple.com/en-us/HT205300.

20. Chris Hall and Dan Grabham, "What Is Bixby? Samsung's Smart Assistant Explained," Pocket-Lint, March 8, 2018, https://www.pocket-lint.com/phones/

news/samsung/140128-what-is-bixby-samsungs-assistant-explained-and-how-to
-use-it.

21. But they may have one by the end of 2018. Chaim Gartenberg, "Samsung's Bixby Smart Speaker Is Coming in the Second Half of 2018," Verge, February 26, 2018, https://www.theverge.com/circuitbreaker/2018/2/26/17053192/samsung -bixby-smart-speaker-home-dj-koh-mwc-2018.

22. Get the Google Assistant app for Android, accessed May 15, 2018, https:// play.google.com/store/apps/details?id=com.google.android.apps. googleassistant&hl=en, and for iOS, accessed May 15, 2018, https://itunes.apple .com/us/app/google-assistant/id1220976145?mt=8.

23. Learn to use Alexa in the Amazon shopping app, accessed May 15, 2018, https://www.amazon.com/gp/help/customer/display.html?nodeId= 202122230.

24. Reverb iOS app, accessed May 15, 2018, https://itunes.apple.com/us/ app/reverb-for-amazon-alexa/id1144695621?mt=8, and Reverb for Android, accessed May 15, 2018, https://play.google.com/store/apps/details?id=agency .rain.android.alexa&hl=en.

25. Cortana for iOS, accessed May 15, 2018, https://itunes.apple.com/us/ app/cortana/id1054501703?mt=8; for Android, accessed May 15, 2018, https:// play.google.com/store/apps/details?id=com.microsoft.cortana&hl=en; and for Windows Phone, accessed May 15, 2018, https://support.microsoft.com/en-za/ help/11694/windows-phone-cortana-on-your-windows-phone.

26. Learn more about Siri on Apple's site, accessed May 15, 2018, https:// www.apple.com/ios/siri/.

27. Amazon's engineers chose the name Alexa because it reminded them of the Library of Alexandria, an inspiration as a place for finding knowledge. They also needed a word that was easy to recognize, and the sound of the X served that purpose. See Julie Bort, "Amazon Engineers Had One Good Reason and One Geeky Reason for Choosing the Name Alexa," Business Insider, July 12, 2016, http://www.businessinsider.com/why-amazon-called-it-alexa-2016-7.

28. Jay McGregor, "Google Assistant Could Get Customizable Hotwords," Forbes, January 31, 2018, https://www.forbes.com/sites/jaymcgregor/2018/01/ 31/google-assistant-could-get-customisable-hotwords/.

29. AnyPod, accessed May 15, 2018, https://www.amazon.com/Harrison -Digital-Media-AnyPod/dp/B072HY3T7Y.

30. Megan Wollerton, "Voice Wars: Siri vs. Alexa vs. Google Assistant," CNET, February 7, 2018, https://www.cnet.com/news/voice-wars-siri-vs-alexa- vs-google-assistant/; Russell Holly, "Amazon Echo vs. Google Home: Which Voice Assistant Answers Questions Best?" Android Central, November 8, 2017, https://www.androidcentral.com/amazon-echo-vs-google-home-questions.

31. Christian Zibreg, "HomePod Cannot Be Used as a Regular Bluetooth Speaker," iDownload Blog, February 2, 2018, http://www.idownloadblog.com/ 2018/02/02/homepod-cannot-be-used-as-a-regular-bluetooth-speaker/.

32. Mike Wuerthele, "How to AirPlay Music to Your HomePod from Spotify, Pandora, Amazon Music, and Apple Music," Apple Insider, February 23, 2018, https://appleinsider.com/articles/18/02/23/how-to-airplay-music-to-your -homepod-from-spotify-pandora-amazon-music-and-apple-music.

33. Craig Lloyd, "How to Listen to Audiobooks on the Amazon Echo," *How-To Geek*, May 19, 2016, https://www.howtogeek.com/253209/how-to-listen-to-audiobooks-on-the-amazon-echo/; Taylor Martin, "How to Listen to Audiobooks on Google Home," CNET, January 23, 2018, https://www.cnet.com/how-to/how-to-listen-to-audiobooks-on-google-home/.

34. See, "Is the Amazon Echo Compatible with the OverDrive App?" on Overdrive's site, accessed May 15, 2018, https://help.overdrive.com/customer/en/portal/articles/2689899-is-the-amazon-echo-compatible-with-the-overdrive-app.

35. Elyse Betters and Max Langridge, "Amazon Alexa Calling and Messaging: What Is It, How Does It Work, and Where Can You Use It?" Pocket-Lint, March 12, 2018, https://www.pocket-lint.com/smart-home/news/amazon/140981-amazon-alexa-calling-and-messaging-what-is-it-how-does-it-work-and-where-can-you-use-it. See also Elyse Betters, "Google Home Calling: How Does It Work and Where Is It Available?" Pocket-Lint, October 4, 2017, https://www.pocket-lint.com/smart-home/news/google/141094-google-home-calling-how-does-it-work-and-where-is-it-available.

36. Michael Gowan and Mike Prospero, "27 Best Alexa Games to Keep You Entertained," *Tom's Guide*, February 2, 2018, https://www.tomsguide.com/us/pictures-story/1070-best-alexa-games.html.

37. Scott Stein, "Google Assistant Uses Joke Writers from Pixar and the Onion," CNET, October 10, 2016, https://www.cnet.com/news/google-hired-pixar-and-onion-joke-writers-for-assistant/.

38. To find some, see Krzysztof Willman, "200+ Funny Amazon Alexa Easter Eggs (Including 100 Hidden Secrets)," TurboFuture, April 19, 2018, https://turbofuture.com/consumer-electronics/200-Amusing-Amazon-Echo-Easter-Eggs; Taylor Martin, "40 Fun Google Home Easter Eggs to Try," CNET, March 8, 2017, https://www.cnet.com/g00/how-to/google-home-fun-easter-eggs-to-try/; Britta O'Boyle, "65 Funny Things to Ask Siri for a Good Giggle," Pocket-Lint, February 8, 2018, https://www.pocket-lint.com/apps/news/apple/134568-funny-things-to-ask-siri-best-things-to-ask-siri-for-a-giggle.

39. Alex Colon and Eric Griffith, "The Best Smart Home Devices of 2018," *PC Magazine*, May 22, 2018, https://www.pcmag.com/article2/0,2817,2410889,00.asp.

40. Mikah Sargent, "These Smart Home Accessories Work with Amazon's Alexa and Apple's HomeKit," iMore, March 6, 2017, https://www.imore.com/these-smart-home-accessories-work-amazons-alexa-and-apples-homekit.

41. IFTTT, "Applets for Voice Assistants," accessed May 15, 2018, https://ifttt.com/collections/voice_assistants.

42. Accessed May 15, 2018, https://ifttt.com/applets/jjWFd4ZP-create-a-note-by-telling-it-to-google-assistant.

43. Accessed May 15, 2018, https://ifttt.com/applets/284243p-tell-alexa-to-email-you-your-shopping-list.

44. Apple didn't allow this at first but announced limited integration with other apps in SiriKit for iOS 11.2. This allows Siri in HomePod to integrate with apps for messaging, lists, and notes. It's possible they will enable more integration in the future. See Zac Hall, "iOS 11.2 Introduces 'SiriKit for HomePod' for Limited Third-Party App Support Using Nearby iPhones or iPads," 9 to 5 Mac, October 30, 2017, https://9to5mac.com/2017/10/30/sirikit-for-homepod-ios-11-2/.

45. See chart in this article. Bret Kinsella, "Amazon Alexa Skill Count Surpasses 30,000 in the U.S.," *Voicebot.ai*, March 22, 2018, https://www.voicebot .ai/2018/03/22/amazon-alexa-skill-count-surpasses-30000-u-s/.

46. Short Bedtime Story, accessed May 15, 2018, https://www.amazon.com/ Webguild-Short-Bedtime-Story/dp/B01DJCJTZ2.

47. Michael Gowan and Mike Prospero, "27 Best Alexa Games to Keep You Entertained," *Tom's Guide*, February 2, 2018, https://www.tomsguide.com/us/ pictures-story/1070-best-alexa-games.html#s1.

48. The Magic Door, accessed May 15, 2018, https://www.amazon.com/The -Magic-Door-LLC/dp/B01BMUU6JQ.

49. Black History Facts, accessed May 15, 2018, https://www.amazon.com/ Amazon-Black-History-Facts/dp/B01MYC6MJG/.

50. Flight Tracker, accessed May 15, 2018, https://www.amazon.com/ Karthik-Balakrishnan-Flight-Tracker/dp/B073TRFLWT/.

51. Kayak, accessed May 15, 2018, https://skills-store.amazon.com/deeplink/ dp/B01EILLOXI?deviceType=app&share&refSuffix=ss_copy.

52. CapitalOne, accessed May 15, 2018, https://www.capitalone.com/ applications/alexa/.

53. Mayo Clinic First Aid, accessed May 15, 2018, https://www.amazon.com/ Mayo-Clinic-First-Aid/dp/B0744LJCV2.

54. Five Minute Workout, accessed May 15, 2018, https://www.amazon.com/ gp/product/B0781CTG58.

55. Bird Song, accessed May 15, 2018, https://www.amazon.com/ Thomptronics-Bird-Song/dp/B01GQGW6P8.

56. NASA Mars, accessed May 15, 2018, https://www.amazon.com/ Jet-Propulsion-Laboratory-NASA-Mars/dp/B01LYTB0MS/.

57. Astronomy Guide, accessed May 15, 2018, https://www.amazon.com/ AJFranke-Astronomy-Guide/dp/B01N4I94CP/.

58. Ask My Buddy, accessed May 15, 2018, https://www.amazon.com/Beach -Dev-Ask-My-Buddy/dp/B017YAF22Y/.

59. Love and Lemons, accessed May 15, 2018, https://www.amazon.com/ Love-and-Lemons/dp/B01MQPMHOF/.

60. My Tesla, accessed May 15, 2018, https://www.amazon.com/Nikhil -Kapur-My-Tesla-Unofficial/dp/B01N9Y4I1E/.

61. Ry Crist, " 'Alexa, Where's My Car?' Automatic Syncs Your Vehicle with Amazon Echo," CNET, November 12, 2015, https://www.cnet.com/news/alexa -where-is-my-car-automatic-syncs-your-vehicle-with-amazon-echo/.

62. Taylor Martin, "50 Most Useful Alexa Skills," CNET, January 29, 2018, https://www.cnet.com/how-to/amazon-echo-most-useful-alexa-skills/.

63. Skill Finder, accessed May 15, 2018, https://www.amazon.com/Amazon -Skill-Finder/dp/B01GGW79U4.

64. Sascha Segan, "Google Assistant Now Has 1,830 Actions: Here They Are," *PC Magazine*, January 24, 2018, https://www.pcmag.com/article/353240/ 200-things-to-ask-your-google-home.

65. Bryan Irace, "Many Siris," Irace.me, February 7, 2018, http://irace.me/siri.

66. Apple's SiriKit, accessed May 15, 2018, https://developer.apple.com/ sirikit/.

67. Edison Research, "The Infinite Dial 2018," SlideShare, March 28, 2018, https://www.slideshare.net/webby2001/infinite-dial-2018.

68. Ibid., slide 60, https://www.slideshare.net/webby2001/infinite-dial-2018/60?src=clipshare.

69. Gartner, "Gartner Reveals Top Predictions for IT Organizations and Users in 2017 and Beyond," press release, October 18, 2016, https://www.gartner.com/newsroom/id/3482117.

70. Dan O'Shea, "Can Google Home Take on Amazon's Echo in 2018?" Retail Dive, January 3, 2018, https://www.retaildive.com/news/can-google-home-take-on-amazons-echo-in-2018/513930/.

71. Bret Kinsella, "Google to Be Smart Speaker Market Share Leader in 2022, HomePod to Pass 20 Million Units," *Voicebot.ai*, February 12, 2018, https://www.voicebot.ai/2018/02/12/google-smart-speaker-market-share-leader-2022-homepod-pass-20-million-units/.

72. NPR and Edison Research, *The Smart Audio Report*, National Public Media, accessed May 15, 2018, https://www.nationalpublicmedia.com/smart-audio-report/.

73. Edison Research, *The Infinite Dial 2018*, March 8, 2018, http://www.edisonresearch.com/infinite-dial-2018/.

74. Find these stats here: accessed May 15, 2018, http://www.slideshare.net/webby2001/infinite-dial-2018.

75. Eufy Genie Smart Speaker with Amazon Alexa, accessed May 15, 2018, https://www.amazon.com/gp/product/B071JN3KYN/.

76. Aarti Shahani, "Voice Recognition Software Finally Beats Humans at Typing, Study Finds," NPR All Tech Considered, August 24, 2016, https://www.npr.org/sections/alltechconsidered/2016/08/24/491156218/voice-recognition-software-finally-beats-humans-at-typing-study-finds.

77. Cathy Pearl, *Designing Voice User Interfaces: Principles of Conversational Experiences* (Sebastopol, CA: O'Reilly Media, 2016), Kindle Edition, Kindle Location 272.

Chapter 2

1. Accessed May 15, 2018, https://www.amazon.com/dp/B06XCM9LJ4/ref=fs_ods_fs_ha_dr.

2. Accessed May 15, 2018, https://www.amazon.com/dp/B01DFKC2SO/ref=fs_ods_fs_aucc_bt.

3. Accessed May 15, 2018, https://www.amazon.com/amazon-echo-dot-kids-edition/dp/B077JFK5YH/.

4. Accessed May 15, 2018, https://www.amazon.com/dp/B01J24C0TI/.

5. Kim Wetzel, "As Amazon and Google Keep Bickering, Consumers Are the Ones Who Lose," Digital Trends, March 6, 2018, https://www.digitaltrends.com/home/how-far-will-amazon-and-google-take-this-bickering-over-youtube-and-nest/.

6. Accessed May 15, 2018, https://www.amazon.com/dp/B073SQYXTW/.

7. Chris Hall, "Amazon Echo Spot Review: That Hits the Spot," Pocket-Lint, January 24, 2018, https://www.pocket-lint.com/smart-home/reviews/amazon/142392-amazon-echo-spot-review-that-hits-the-spot.

8. Accessed May 15, 2018, https://www.amazon.com/dp/B075RPT9WT/.

9. Accessed May 15, 2018, https://www.amazon.com/dp/B0186JAEWK/.

10. Thuy Ong, "Amazon's Echo Look Style Assistant Gets a Little Bit Smarter," Verge, February 7, 2018, https://www.theverge.com/2018/2/7/16984218/amazons-echo-look-collections-feature-curated-content-vogue-gq.

11. Jon Kalish, "Why Amazon's Alexa Is "Life Changing" for the Blind," *PC Magazine*, January 8, 2018, https://www.pcmag.com/news/358338/why-amazons-alexa-is-life-changing-for-the-blind.

12. Amazon Tap, accessed May 15, 2018, https://www.amazon.com/Amazon-Tap-Portable-Wireless-Bluetooth-Speaker-with-WiFi-Alexa/dp/B01BH83OOM/. See also Nicole Edsall, "How Different Are the Amazon Tap and the Amazon Echo Really?" Digital Trends, August 24, 2018, https://www.digitaltrends.com/home/amazon-echo-vs-amazon-tap/.

13. Accessed May 15, 2018, https://www.amazon.com/b/?ie=UTF8&node=6669703011.

14. Accessed May 15, 2018, https://store.google.com/product/google_home.

15. Taylor Martin, "How to Customize the Appearance of Google Home," CNET, January 10, 2017, https://www.cnet.com/how-to/how-to-customize-the-appearance-of-google-home/.

16. Accessed May 15, 2018, https://store.google.com/product/google_home_mini.

17. Timothy J. Seppala, "Chromecast Audio Connects Your Existing Speakers for $35," *Engadget*, September 29, 2015, https://www.engadget.com/2015/09/29/google-chromecast-audio/.

18. Accessed May 15, 2018, https://store.google.com/us/product/google_home_max.

19. Kellen, "Here Are the Google Assistant Speakers with Smart Displays," Droid Life, January 9, 2018, https://www.droid-life.com/2018/01/09/google-assistant-speakers-smart-displays/.

20. "Seeing Is Believing on the New Lenovo™ Smart Display—with the Google Assistant™ Built In," *Lenovo Blog*, January 8, 2018, http://blog.lenovo.com/en/blog/seeing-is-believing-on-the-new-lenovo-smart-display-with-the-google-assista.

21. According to David Pogue, in "Apple's HomePod Speaker: Either Way Late or Way Early," Yahoo Finance, February 7, 2018, https://finance.yahoo.com/news/apples-homepod-speaker-either-way-late-way-early-234238812.html, "The audio quality will floor you. Let's just get one thing straight: The HomePod sounds better than the Google Home Max ($400), the Sonos One ($200), or the Amazon Echo Plus ($150), let alone all the smaller Echos and Google Homes. This isn't a matter of opinion; it seems to be a universal consensus among critics, and also my own reaction."

22. Chris Velazco, "Apple HomePod Review: A Great Speaker That's Not So Smart," *Engadget*, February 13, 2018, https://www.engadget.com/2018/02/13/apple-homepod-review/.

23. Accessed May 15, 2018, https://www.apple.com/homepod/.

24. Mikah Sargent and Serenity Caldwell, "HomeKit: The Ultimate Guide to Apple Home Automation," iMore, February 12, 2018, https://www.imore.com/homekit.

25. Ryan Christoffel, "What HomePod Should Become: A Hub for All Apple-Centric Needs," MacStories, March 15, 2018, https://www.macstories.net/stories/what-homepod-should-become-a-hub-for-all-apple-centric-needs/.

26. Valentina Palladino, "Harman Kardon Invoke Review: Cortana Isn't Too Comfortable in the Home Yet," Ars Technica, October 30, 2017, https://arstechnica.com/gadgets/2017/10/harman-kardon-invoke-review-cortana-isnt-too-comfortable-in-the-home-yet/.

27. Todd Haselton, "Microsoft's Noble Attempt at a Smart Speaker Isn't as Good as the Google Home or Amazon Echo," CNBC, October 20, 2017, https://www.cnbc.com/2017/10/20/microsoft-invoke-speaker-review.html.

28. Rachel Cericola, "The Best Alexa-Compatible Smart-Home Devices for Amazon Echo," Wirecutter, November 3, 2017, https://thewirecutter.com/reviews/best-alexa-compatible-smart-home-devices-for-amazon-echo/.

29. Ry Crist, "Alexa? HomeKit? Google Home? These Gizmos Work with All Three," CNET, July 17, 2017, https://www.cnet.com/pictures/alexa-homekit-google-home-these-smart-gadgets-work-with-all-three/.

30. Use Siri on your Apple TV 4K or Apple TV (4th generation), accessed May 15, 2018, https://support.apple.com/en-us/HT205300. For now, you need the Siri Remote for voice control; using a HomePod for that purpose is not fully functional. See Benjamin Mayo, "How to Use HomePod with Apple TV ... It Mostly Works, but There Are Some Drawbacks," 9 to 5 Mac, February 11, 2018, https://9to5mac.com/2018/02/11/how-to-use-homepod-with-apple-tv/.

31. "Play TV Shows & Movies Using Google Home," Google Home Help, accessed May 15, 2018, https://support.google.com/googlehome/answer/7214982?hl=en; Chromecast, accessed May 15, 2018, https://store.google.com/product/chromecast_2015.

32. "Fire TV Stick with Alexa Voice Remote," accessed May 15, 2018, https://www.amazon.com/dp/B00ZV9RDKK/; "Fire TV with 4K Ultra HD and Alexa Voice Remote," accessed May 15, 2018, https://www.amazon.com/dp/B01N32NCPM.

33. Ashley Carman, "You Can Now Use Alexa to Control Amazon's Fire TV without a Remote," Verge, August 1, 2017, https://www.theverge.com/circuitbreaker/2017/8/1/16075272/amazon-fire-tv-echo-voice-control-alexa.

34. Sean Hollister, "Alexa Can Control Your TV with a Logitech Harmony. Here's How," CNET, July 19, 2017, https://www.cnet.com/how-to/how-to-logitech-harmony-amazon-alexa-echo/.

35. Barb Gonzalez, "TV Voice Control: Google Assistant vs. Amazon Alexa," Sound & Vision, July 14, 2017, https://www.soundandvision.com/content/hands-video-command-google-home-and-amazon-alexa.

36. Sarah Perez, "Alexa Support Comes to 2018 TVs from Sony, Hisense and LG," TechCrunch, January 9, 2018, https://techcrunch.com/2018/01/08/alexa-support-comes-to-2018-tvs-from-sony-and-hisense/.

37. Scott Scrivens, "Sony Announces New 4K HDR Android TVs with Google Assistant Built In," Android Police, March 26, 2018, https://www.androidpolice.com/2018/02/08/sony-announces-new-4k-hdr-android-tvs-google-assistant-built/.

38. Lory Gil, "Here's What Siri Will and Won't Do on the Apple TV," iMore, August 21, 2017, https://www.imore.com/what-can-siri-do-apple-tv.

39. Ben Popper, "Google Is Pulling YouTube off the Fire TV and Echo Show as Feud with Amazon Grows," Verge, December 5, 2017, https://www.theverge.com/2017/12/5/16738748/google-amazon-feud-youtube-pulled-off-fire-tv-echo-show-nest-devices.

40. Nat Levy, "Sorry, Google: We Tried Amazon's YouTube Workaround on Fire TV, and It Worked Great," GeekWire, January 2, 2018, https://www.geekwire.com/2018/sorry-google-tried-amazons-youtube-workaround-fire-tv-worked-great/.

41. Parker Hall, "How to Watch Amazon Instant Video on Chromecast or Android TV," Digital Trends, March 8, 2018, https://www.digitaltrends.com/home-theater/how-to-watch-amazon-instant-video-on-chromecast-or-android-tv/.

42. Rik Henderson, "Amazon Fire TV Tips and Tricks: How to Get the Most from Your Fire TV Stick or 4K Box," Pocket-Lint, December 25, 2017, https://www.pocket-lint.com/tv/news/amazon/140966-amazon-fire-tv-tips-and-tricks-how-to-get-the-most-from-your-fire-tv-stick-or-4k-box.

43. Nathan Ingraham, "Amazon Echo Show Review: Seeing Is Believing," Engadget, June 26, 2017, https://www.engadget.com/2017/06/26/amazon-echo-show-review/.

44. Accessed May 15, 2018, https://www.jibo.com/.

45. Accessed May 15, 2018, https://www.heykuri.com/.

46. Sony's Aibo (robot puppy) can do tricks, show emotions with its body language, recognize different people in your family, and be trained over time. Eventually it will include smart home features, similar to those offered by Alexa or Google Assistant. For more information, accessed May 15, 2018, see https://aibo.sony.jp/en/.

47. "Jibo the Robot Still Has a Lot to Learn from Alexa," Boston Globe YouTube channel, accessed May 15, 2018, https://youtu.be/Blhovhmv1yA.

48. See an interview with Cynthia Breazeal, founder of Jibo, accessed May 15, 2018, on https://www.jibo.com/.

49. Team Jibo, "Be a Maker—Companion App for Jibo Is Here!" Jibo Blog, April 12, 2018, https://blog.jibo.com/be-a-maker.

50. Khari Johnson, "Toyota Is Bringing Alexa to Select Vehicles This Year," VentureBeat, January 9, 2018, https://venturebeat.com/2018/01/09/toyota-is-bringing-alexa-to-select-vehicles-this-year/.

51. Khari Johnson, "5 CES 2018 Announcements That Put Alexa inside Cars," VentureBeat, January 13, 2018, https://venturebeat.com/2018/01/13/5-ces-announcements-that-put-alexa-inside-cars/.

52. Bret Kinsella, "Google Assistant Now Available on Android Auto," Voicebot.ai, January 10, 2018, https://www.voicebot.ai/2018/01/10/google-assistant-now-available-android-auto/.

53. Accessed May 15, 2018, https://www.automatic.com/apps/amazon-echo/.

54. Accessed May 15, 2018, https://www.automatic.com/pro/.

55. Ry Crist, " 'Alexa, Where's My Car?' Automatic Syncs Your Vehicle with Amazon Echo," CNET, November 12, 2015, https://www.cnet.com/news/alexa -where-is-my-car-automatic-syncs-your-vehicle-with-amazon-echo/; Eric Ravenscraft, "How to Connect Automatic Pro to Alexa and Talk to Your Car," *How-To Geek*, May 4, 2017, https://www.howtogeek.com/305057/how-to-connect-automatic-pro -to-alexa-and-talk-to-your-car/.

56. Cork Gaines, "Toyota Is Adding Amazon's Alexa to Cars: We've Been Using Alexa in a Car for 6 Months and It's the Best Infotainment System We've Ever Used," Business Insider, January 10, 2018, http://www.businessinsider.com/ using-amazon-echo-dot-in-a-car-2017-7.

57. Lindsey Banks, "The Complete Guide to Hearable Technology in 2018," Everyday Hearing, June 13, 2018, https://www.everydayhearing.com/hearing -technology/articles/hearables/.

58. Josh Smith, "3 Reasons to Wait for AirPods 2 & 4 Reasons Not To," Gotta Be Mobile, June 21, 2018, https://www.gottabemobile.com/reasons-to-wait-for -airpods-2-reasons-not-to/.

59. Sherri L. Smith, "Jabra Elite 65t Wireless Earbuds Review: A True AirPod Killer," *Tom's Guide*, March 14, 2018, https://www.tomsguide.com/us/jabra-elite -65t-wireless-earbuds,review-5215.html.

60. Sean O'Kane, "Google Pixel Buds Review: The Future Shouldn't Be This Awkward," Verge, November 16, 2017, https://www.theverge.com/2017/11/16/ 16659314/google-pixel-buds-review-bluetooth-headphones.

61. Heather Kelly, "Review: Google Pixel Buds Falls Short of Promise," CNN Tech, November 22, 2017, http://money.cnn.com/2017/11/20/technology/ google-pixel-buds-review/index.html.

62. Accessed May 15, 2018, https://www.smartear.ai/.

63. Plot summary of the movie *Her*, from IMDb, accessed May 15, 2018, https://www.imdb.com/title/tt1798709/plotsummary.

64. See these, for example. Bret Kinsella, "Siri Does Better Than Expected in Voice Assistant Face Off, But Google Still Leads,"*Voicebot.ai*, February 12, 2018, https://www.voicebot.ai/2018/02/12/siri-better-expected-voice-assistant-face -off-google-still-leads/; Dan Moren, "Alexa vs. Google Assistant vs. Siri: Google Widens Its Lead," *Tom's Guide*, June 4, 2018, https://www.tomsguide.com/us/ alexa-vs-siri-vs-google,review-4772.html; Grant Clauser, "Amazon Echo vs. Google Home: Which Voice Controlled Speaker Is Best for You?" Wirecutter, June 8, 2018, https://thewirecutter.com/reviews/amazon-echo-vs-google-home/.

65. Grant Clauser, "What Is Alexa? What Is the Amazon Echo, and Should You Get One?" Wirecutter, June 7, 2018, https://thewirecutter.com/reviews/what-is -alexa-what-is-the-amazon-echo-and-should-you-get-one.

66. An Amazon Echo that circulates at the Framingham Public Library, accessed May 15, 2018, https://framinghamlibrary.org/amazon-echo.

67. Sarah Perez, "Storyline Lets You Build and Publish Alexa Skills without Coding," TechCrunch, February 3, 2018, https://techcrunch.com/2018/02/02/ storyline-lets-you-build-and-publish-alexa-skills-without-coding/.

68. Sonia Tan, "The Complete Step-By-Step Guide to Getting Your Amazon Alexa Skill Live," WisQo, April 28, 2107, https://www.wisqo.com/single-post/2017/ 04/28/The-complete-step-by-step-guide-to-getting-your-Amazon-Alexa-skill-live.

69. Accessed May 15, 2018, https://developer.amazon.com/alexa-skills-kit.

70. Accessed May 15, 2018, https://www.amazon.com/Darian-Johnson-Black-History-Facts/dp/B01JL5H21O/.

71. Accessed May 15, 2018, https://www.amazon.com/gp/product/B074DFXV2Z/.

72. Lorrie Pearson, "How I Programmed My First Amazon Alexa Skill and Won a Free Echo Dot," freeCodeCamp, August 11, 2017, https://medium.freecodecamp.org/how-to-use-your-tech-skill-to-create-alexa-skills-a3e9f210a952.

73. Hugh Langley, "What It's Like to Build an Alexa Skill—and How You Can Do It Yourself," Ambient, January 4, 2018, https://www.the-ambient.com/how-to/how-to-build-an-alexa-skill-197.

74. Accessed May 15, 2018, https://www.sayspring.com/.

75. Pricing for Storyline, accessed May 15, 2018, https://getstoryline.com/pricing; pricing for Sayspring, accessed May 15, 2018, https://www.sayspring.com/product/#sayspring-pricing.

76. Google, "Build Actions for the Google Assistant with Actions on Google," accessed May 15, 2018, https://developers.google.com/actions/.

77. Tom Hudson, "How to Build Your Own Action for Google Home Using API.AI," Smashing Magazine, May 29, 2017, https://www.smashingmagazine.com/2017/05/build-action-google-home-api-ai/; Jonathan Eisenzopf, "Building Your First Action for Google Home (in 30 minutes)," Medium, April 5, 2017, https://medium.com/google-cloud/building-your-first-action-for-google-home-in-30-minutes-ec6c65b7bd32.

78. Corbin Davenport, "Google Is Offering up to $10,000 to Developers Making Google Assistant Actions," Android Police, May 29, 2017, https://www.androidpolice.com/2017/05/29/google-offering-prizes-developers-making-google-assistant-actions/.

79. Amazon, "Earn Money with Alexa Developer Rewards," accessed May 15, 2018, https://developer.amazon.com/alexa-skills-kit/rewards.

80. Categories of skills eligible for developer rewards are education and reference; food and drink; games, trivia, and accessories; health and fitness; kids; lifestyle; music and audio; and productivity.

81. Ben Fox Rubin, "What Amazon's Alexa Economy Pays the People Building Its Skills," CNET, December 26, 2017, https://www.cnet.com/news/amazon-alexa-economy-echo-speaker-google-assistant-siri/.

82. Alistair Charlton, "Alexa, Bring Me Pizza: 7 Ways to Order Take Out and Coffee with Your Amazon Echo," Gearbrain, February 15, 2018, https://www.gearbrain.com/alexa-skills-for-ordering-takeout-2534882363.html.

Chapter 3

1. Taylor Martin, "12 Ways to Use Alexa in the Kitchen," CNET, November 20, 2017, https://www.cnet.com/how-to/amazon-echo-ways-to-use-alexa-in-the-kitchen/.

2. Accessed May 15, 2018, https://www.baby-stats.com/.

3. Carlos Cheung, "An Echo Never Forgets: Taking Care of Your Newborn with Baby Stats," VoiceLabs.co, July 25, 2017, http://voicelabs.co/2017/07/25/an-echo-never-forgets/.

4. For more ideas, see Didier Thizy, "Amazon's Alexa Voice Service in Healthcare," *Macadamian Blog*, June 29, 2016, http://www.macadamian.com/2016/06/29/amazons-alexa-voice-service-in-healthcare/.

5. Jordan Crook, "Amazon Is Putting Alexa in the Office," TechCrunch, November 30, 2017, https://techcrunch.com/2017/11/29/amazon-is-putting-alexa-in-the-office/.

6. Jordan Crook, "WeWork Has Big Plans for Alexa for Business," TechCrunch, November 30, 2017, https://techcrunch.com/2017/11/30/wework-has-big-plans-for-alexa-for-business/.

7. Trefis Team, "How Amazon Is Looking to Make Alexa a Workplace Assistant," *Forbes*, March 7, 2017, https://www.forbes.com/sites/greatspeculations/2017/03/07/how-amazon-is-looking-to-make-alexa-a-workplace-assistant/.

8. Taylor Soper, "Testing Alexa in a Hotel Room: We Used Amazon's Voice Assistant inside a Swanky Las Vegas Suite," GeekWire, January 10, 2018, https://www.geekwire.com/2018/testing-alexa-hotel-room-used-amazons-voice-assistant-inside-swanky-las-vegas-suite/.

9. David K. Gibson, "The Always-On Digital Assistant Comes to Your Hotel Room," *Afar*, September 27, 2017, https://www.afar.com/magazine/the-always-on-digital-assistant-with-big-ears-comes-to-your-hotel-room.

10. Elizabeth Woyke, "The Octogenarians Who Love Amazon's Alexa," *MIT Technology Review*, June 9, 2017, https://www.technologyreview.com/s/608047/the-octogenarians-who-love-amazons-alexa/.

11. Aaron Mizak, Megan Park, Davis Park, and Kari Olson, *Amazon "Alexa" Pilot Analysis Report*, Front Porch Center for Innovation and Wellbeing, December 2017, http://fpciw.org/wp-content/uploads/sites/15/2017/12/FINAL-DRAFT-Amazon-Alexa-Analysis-Report.pdf.

12. Ibid., p. 13.

13. "How Echo Can Help Care for Aging or Disabled Family Members," *Love My Echo*, January 22, 2016, https://lovemyecho.com/2016/01/22/how-echo-can-help-care-for-aging-or-disabled-family-members/.

14. Sophie Gidley, "Smart Speaker Technology Trial to Aid Supported Living," BBC News, November 19, 2017, http://www.bbc.com/news/uk-wales-south-east-wales-42029859; Cathy Pearl, "The Societal Benefits of Smart Speakers," *VUI Magazine*, April 2, 2018, https://medium.com/vui-magazine/the-societal-benefits-of-smart-speakers-274073cfe7ae.

15. Anna Schaverien, "Amazon Echo—My Blind Dad's New Best Friend," *Memo*, August 1, 2017, https://www.thememo.com/2017/08/01/blind-dad-tried-amazon-echo-now-loves-alexa/.

16. Luis Pérez, "Amazon Echo as an Accessibility Support," The Website of Luis Pérez, December 5, 2016, https://luisperezonline.com/2016/12/05/amazon-echo-as-an-accessibility-support/.

17. Echo Look, accessed May 15, 2018, https://www.amazon.com/dp/B0186JAEWK.

18. They do this by a combination of machine-learning algorithms and advice from fashion specialists. Learn more in Tom Brant, "Amazon Look Is a Camera That Picks Your Outfit," *PC Magazine*, April 26, 2017, https://www.pcmag.com/news/353322/amazon-look-is-a-camera-that-picks-your-outfit.

19. Jon Kalish, "Why Amazon's Alexa Is 'Life Changing' for the Blind," *PC Magazine*, January 8, 2018, https://www.pcmag.com/news/358338/why-amazons-alexa-is-life-changing-for-the-blind.

20. Grubhub skill for Alexa, accessed May 15, 2018, https://www.amazon.com/Grubhub-Reorder-with/dp/B01N6ZZQDO.

21. Peapod skill for Alexa, accessed May 15, 2018, https://www.amazon.com/Peapod-LLC-Ask/dp/B072N8GFZ3/.

22. "How Tecla-E Enhances Amazon Alexa for Quadriplegic Users," Tecla, June 13, 2017, https://gettecla.com/blogs/news/how-tecla-e-enhances-amazon-alexa-for-users-with-physical-disabilities.

23. Luis Pérez, "Amazon Echo as an Accessibility Support," The Website of Luis Pérez, December 5, 2016, https://luisperezonline.com/2016/12/05/amazon-echo-as-an-accessibility-support/.

24. "Augmentative and Alternative Communication (AAC)," American Speech-Language-Hearing Association, accessed May 15, 2018,https://www.asha.org/public/speech/disorders/aac/.

25. Proloquo4Text, accessed May 15, 2018, https://itunes.apple.com/us/app/proloquo4text/id751646884?mt=8.

26. "Why Voiceitt?" Voiceitt, accessed May 15, 2018, http://www.voiceitt.com/why-voiceitt.html.

27. Bret Kinsella, "2018 Voice Assistant Predictions from 20 Innovators," *Voicebot.ai*, December 20, 2017, https://www.voicebot.ai/2017/12/20/2018-voice-assistant-predictions-20-innovators/.

28. Gwyneth A. Jones, "There's an Echo in My Library!" Daring Librarian, June 14, 2015, https://www.thedaringlibrarian.com/2015/06/echo-in-my-library.html.

29. Ibid.

30. Sarah FitzHenry, "Google Home in the School Library: FAQ," Fitz between the Shelves, January 30, 2017, https://fitzbetweentheshelves.com/2017/01/30/google-home-in-the-school-library-faq/.

31. See her presentation slides here: accessed May 15, 2018, https://docs.google.com/presentation/d/13LkIKDnz_l-KwZUmLE-RvYPLPABePVUto27HpU-xp0U/edit.

32. Sarah FitzHenry, "Google Home in the School Library: FAQ," Fitz between the Shelves, January 20, 2017, https://fitzbetweentheshelves.com/2017/01/30/google-home-in-the-school-library-faq/.

33. Ibid.

34. "Using the Amazon Echo Dot and Alexa in the Classroom," *Erin*tegration*, December 26, 2016, http://www.erintegration.com/2016/12/26/amazon-echo-dot-and-alexa-in-the-classroom/.

35. Ibid.

36. Vicki Davis, "Amazon Alexa in the Classroom, Episode 108 with Bill Selak," *The CoolCat Teacher*, accessed May 15, 2018, http://www.coolcatteacher.com/amazon-alexa-classroom/.

37. Ibid.

38. Lauren Barack, "'Alexa, Can We Go to School Today?'" Education Dive, February 21, 2018, https://www.educationdive.com/news/alexa-can-we-go-to -school-today/517547/.

39. Kate Roddy, "Alexa, How Can You Improve Teaching and Learning?" EdScoop, December 19, 2017, https://edscoop.com/voice-command-technology -alexa-how-can-you-improve-teaching-and-learning.

40. Amazon Echo, accessed May 15, 2018, https://framinghamlibrary.org/ amazon-echo; Google Home, accessed May 15, 2018, https://framinghamlibrary .org/google-home.

41. Jesusa Christians, "Alexa Provides a New Resource Tool to the Missouri Valley Public Library," *Missouri Valley Times-News*, September 14, 2016, http:// www.enterprisepub.com/movalley/news/alexa-provides-a-new-resource-tool-to -the-missouri-valley/article_fc739dd0-7a82-11e6-b694-3b99d28d9504.html.

42. "Amazon's Alexa," Grande Prairie Public Library, accessed May 15, 2018, https://www.grandeprairie.org/events/amazons-alexa/.

43. "Never Too Late to Learn: Tech for Seniors—Google Home vs. Amazon Echo—Main," Tuscarawas County Public Library System, accessed May 15, 2018, https://www.tusclibrary.org/content/never-too-late-learn-tech-seniors-google-home -vs-amazon-echo-main.

44. "Amazon Alexa Voice Services Bootcamp—Session 2," Eventbrite, accessed May 15, 2018, https://www.eventbrite.com/e/amazon-alexa-voice -services-bootcamp-session-2-tickets-33098498500#. From the description: "As part of Maker Faire Westport, Remarkable STEAM, in partnership with the Westport Library, is pleased to announce an Amazon Alexa Skills Building Bootcamp on Sunday, April 23, 2017. Alexa, the voice service that powers Amazon Echo, provides capabilities, or skills, that enable customers to interact with devices in a more intuitive way using their own voice."

45. L.A. Public Library Blog (flash briefing skill) , accessed May 15, 2018, https://www.amazon.com/dp/B0784WMYB5; L.A. Public Library Hot Fiction, accessed May 15, 2018, https://www.amazon.com/L-A-Public-Library-Hot-Fiction/ dp/B077SZ3TPV.

46. Houston Library, accessed May 15, 2018, https://www.amazon.com/ Chris-Houston-Library/dp/B0794MXF4D/.

47. Toronto Library Unofficial, accessed May 15, 2018, https://www.amazon .com/Pavol-Zibrita-Toronto-library-unofficial/dp/B01M3N6GFX/.

48. "Alexa Skill," Worthington Libraries, June 15, 2018, https://www .worthingtonlibraries.org/visit/services/alexa-skill.

49. Ibid.

50. Burbio, accessed May 15, 2018, http://www.burbio.com/states.

51. Burbio skill, accessed May 15, 2018, https://www.amazon.com/Burbio/ dp/B01MRAGMKW.

52. "Ask Alexa 'What's Happening at the Pompton Lakes Library?'" The Free Public Library of the Borough of Pompton Lakes, August 22, 2017, https:// www.pomptonlakeslibrary.org/ask-alexa-whats-happening-at-the-pompton-lakes -library/.

53. "Equipment and Technology: Equipment," Vogel Library, Wartburg College, accessed May 15, 2018, http://knightguides.wartburg.edu/equipntech/equipment.

54. IowaStateLibFacts skill, accessed May 15, 2018, https://www.amazon.com/Iowa-State-University-Library-IowaStateLibFacts/dp/B07BH2DXW9.

55. CSUSB News skill, accessed May 15, 2018, https://www.amazon.com/CSUSB-News/dp/B074WRD8TK/.

56. See MIT Facts by Massachusetts Institute of Technology (MIT) , accessed May 15, 2018, https://www.amazon.com/Massachusetts-Institute-of-Technology-MIT/dp/B07BJ8T5W7/; Lehigh University by Lehigh University, accessed May 15, 2018, https://www.amazon.com/Lehigh-University/dp/B01MYG94E1/; The Ohio State Skill by The Ohio State University, accessed May 15, 2018, https://www.amazon.com/The-Ohio-State-University-Skill/dp/B01KQX4T3E/; University of San Diego by USD Developer Account, accessed May 15, 2018, https://www.amazon.com/USD-Developer-Account-University-Diego/dp/B01MSHH1KS; OU Facts by The University of Oklahoma, accessed May 15, 2018, https://www.amazon.com/The-University-of-Oklahoma-Facts/dp/B01N7WBM48/; OU Directory by The University of Oklahoma, accessed May 15, 2018, https://www.amazon.com/The-University-of-Oklahoma-Directory/dp/B073WL5BYR/.

57. "ASU, Amazon Bring First-of-Its-Kind Voice-Technology Program to Campus," *ASU Now*, August 17 2017, https://asunow.asu.edu/20170817-asu-news-asu-amazon-dots-tooker-house.

58. Matt Weinberger, "Amazon Donated 1,600 Echo Dot Smart Speakers to ASU's New High-Tech Dorm for Engineers," Business Insider, August 17, 2017, http://www.businessinsider.com/amazon-echo-dot-asu-tooker-house-fulton-schools-engineering-2017-8.

59. Arizona State University skill, accessed May 15, 2018, https://www.amazon.com/Arizona-State-University-Events-Hours/dp/B074RCQRN8/.

60. Bertrand Vacherot, "University of Oklahoma Expands Student Engagement with Alexa Skills," *Alexa Blogs*, December 28, 2017, https://developer.amazon.com/blogs/alexa/post/b9411ff3-02c4-47d5-acea-062c0bf0fd63/university-of-oklahoma-expands-student-engagement-with-alexa-skills.

61. Douglas Booms, "Amazon Launches Alexa Fund Fellowship to Help University Students Create the Next Big Thing in Voice," *Alexa Blogs*, March 2, 2017, https://developer.amazon.com/blogs/post/db400b81-d851-405a-9b92-3fef4458d0da/amazon-launches-alexa-fund-fellowship-to-help-university-students-create-the-next-big-thing-in-voice.

62. Ashwin Ram, "University of Washington Students Win Inaugural Alexa Prize," *Alexa Blogs*, November 28, 2017, https://developer.amazon.com/blogs/alexa/post/1a6a19d8-e45d-4b3b-981d-776a378ba625/university-of-washington-students-win-inaugural-alexa-prize.

63. James Vlahos, "Inside the Alexa Prize," *Wired*, February 27, 2018, https://www.wired.com/story/inside-amazon-alexa-prize/.

64. See Chapter 7, "Experimenting," in Nicole Hennig, *Keeping Up with Emerging Technologies: Best Practices for Information Professionals* (Santa Barbara, CA: Libraries Unlimited, 2017).

Chapter 4

1. Jaime Green, "How to Delete the Voice Data That Amazon Echo and Google Home Are Storing," *Lifehacker*, November 26, 2017, https://lifehacker.com/how-to-delete-the-voice-data-that-amazon-echo-and-googl-1820737802.

2. Tim Moynihan, "Alexa and Google Home Record What You Say. But What Happens to That Data?" *Wired*, December 5, 2016, https://www.wired.com/2016/12/alexa-and-google-record-your-voice/.

3. Jacob Kleinman, "How to Protect Your Privacy on Your Smart Home Devices," *Lifehacker*, February 21, 2018, https://lifehacker.com/how-to-protect-your-privacy-on-your-smart-home-devices-1823181500.

4. Jason Cipriani, "Google Home: 12 Tips and Tricks to Get Started," CNET, May 22, 2017, https://www.cnet.com/how-to/google-home-tips-and-tricks/.

5. Rene Ritchie, "How to Turn Off and Customize 'Hey Siri' on HomePod," iMore, February 8, 2018, https://www.imore.com/how-customize-hey-siri-homepod.

6. Jacob Kleinman, "How to Protect Your Privacy on Your Smart Home Devices," *Lifehacker*, February 21, 2018, https://lifehacker.com/how-to-protect-your-privacy-on-your-smart-home-devices-1823181500.

7. Ibid.

8. "Manage Voice Purchasing Settings," Amazon Help, accessed May 15, 2018, https://www.amazon.com/gp/help/customer/display.html?nodeId=201952610.

9. Jay Stanley, "The Privacy Threat from Always-On Microphones like the Amazon Echo," *ACLU Blog*, January 13, 2017, https://www.aclu.org/blog/privacy-technology/privacy-threat-always-microphones-amazon-echo.

10. John Patrick Pullen, "It's Finally (Sort of) Legal for Kids to Use an Amazon Echo, Says FTC," *Fortune*, October 24, 2017, http://fortune.com/2017/10/24/amazon-echo-alexa-children-kids-privacy/.

11. Federal Trade Commission, "FTC Provides Additional Guidance on COPPA and Voice Recordings," press release, October 23, 2017, https://www.ftc.gov/news-events/press-releases/2017/10/ftc-provides-additional-guidance-coppa-voice-recordings.

12. Bret Kinsella, "Amazon Now Allows Alexa Skills for Kids," *Voicebot.ai*, September 5, 2017, https://www.voicebot.ai/2017/09/05/amazon-now-allows-alexa-skills-kids/.

13. "Google Home & Your Child's Google Account," Google for Families Help, accessed May 15, 2018, https://support.google.com/families/answer/7521263?hl=en.

14. "Family Disclosure for Parents," Google Family Link, accessed May 15, 2018, https://families.google.com/familylink/privacy/notice/.

15. "Tips for Families," Google Family Link, accessed May 15, 2018, https://families.google.com/familylink/family-tips/.

16. Echo Dot Kids Edition, accessed May 15, 2018, https://www.amazon.com/amazon-echo-dot-kids-edition/dp/B077JFK5YH.

17. Jillian D'Onfro, "As Apple Gets Slammed for Addictive Smartphones, Experts Are Optimistic about the Amazon Echo and Google Home," CNBC,

January 14, 2018, https://www.cnbc.com/2018/01/14/effect-of-smart-assistants
-like-amazon-echo-google-home-on-kids.html.

18. Matt Rosoff, "Survey Spells Trouble for Apple and Samsung: People
with Devices like Amazon Echo Use Phones Less," CNBC, January 7, 2018,
https://www.cnbc.com/2018/01/06/amazon-echo-and-other-assistants-often-lower
-smartphone-use.html.

19. Rachel Metz, "Growing Up with Alexa," *MIT Technology Review*,
August 16, 2017, https://www.technologyreview.com/s/608430/growing-up
-with-alexa/.

20. Stefania Druga, Randi Williams, Cynthia Breazeal, and Mitchel Resnick,
"'Hey Google Is It OK If I Eat You?': Initial Explorations in Child-Agent
Interaction," *IDC '17 Proceedings of the 2017 Conference on Interaction Design and
Children* (Stanford, CA, June 27–30, 2017, pp. 595–600), https://dl.acm.org/
citation.cfm?id=3084330.

21. Ibid.

22. Team Jibo, "Be a Maker—Companion App for Jibo is Here!" *Jibo Blog*,
April 12, 2018, https://blog.jibo.com/be-a-maker.

23. Soapbox Labs, accessed May 15, 2018, http://www.soapboxlabs.com/.

24. Andy Boxall, "Voice Recognition for Kids Isn't Child's Play, but This
Company Has Mastered It," Digital Trends, December 22, 2017, https://www
.digitaltrends.com/mobile/soapbox-voice-recognition-for-kids-news/.

25. Chandra Steele, "The Real Reason Voice Assistants Are Female (and Why It
Matters)," *PC Magazine*, January 4, 2018, https://www.pcmag.com/commentary/
358057/the-real-reason-voice-assistants-are-female-and-why-it-matt.

26. Sarah Zhang, "No, Women's Voices Are Not Easier to Understand Than
Men's Voices," Gizmodo, February 5, 2015, https://gizmodo.com/no-siri-is-not
-female-because-womens-voices-are-easier-1683901643.

27. Wade J. Mitchell, Chin-Chang Ho, Himalaya Patel, and Karl F.
MacDorman, "Does Social Desirability Bias Favor Humans? Explicit–Implicit
Evaluations of Synthesized Speech Support a New HCI Model of Impression
Management," *Computers in Human Behavior* 27, no. 1 (2011): 402–412, http://
www.macdorman.com/kfm/writings/pubs/Mitchell2010DoesSocialDesirability
BiasFavorHumans.pdf.

28. Megan Garber, "Why We Prefer Masculine Voices (Even in Women),"
Atlantic, December 18, 2012, https://www.theatlantic.com/sexes/archive/2012/
12/why-we-prefer-masculine-voices-even-in-women/266350/.

29. Clifford Nass and Scott Brave, *Wired for Speech: How Voice Activates and
Advances the Human-Computer Relationship* (Cambridge, MA: MIT Press, 2005),
https://mitpress.mit.edu/books/wired-speech.

30. Chandra Steele, "The Real Reason Voice Assistants Are Female (and Why It
Matters)," *PC Magazine*, January 4, 2018, https://www.pcmag.com/commentary/
358057/the-real-reason-voice-assistants-are-female-and-why-it-matt.

31. Leah Fessler, "We Tested Bots like Siri and Alexa to See Who Would
Stand Up to Sexual Harassment," Quartz, February 22, 2017, https://qz.com/
911681/we-tested-apples-siri-amazon-echos-alexa-microsofts-cortana-and-googles
-google-home-to-see-which-personal-assistant-bots-stand-up-for-themselves-in-the
-face-of-sexual-harassment/.

32. Cosette Jarrett, "Petition Asks Siri and Alexa to Flip the Script on Sexual Harassment," VentureBeat, December 8, 2017, https://venturebeat.com/2017/12/08/petition-asks-siri-and-alexa-to-flip-the-script-on-sexual-harassment/.

33. Leah Fessler, "Amazon's Alexa Is Now a Feminist, and She's Sorry If That Upsets You," Quartz at Work, January 17, 2018, https://work.qz.com/1180607/amazons-alexa-is-now-a-feminist-and-shes-sorry-if-that-upsets-you/.

34. Madeline Buxton, "Writing for Alexa Becomes More Complicated in the #MeToo Era," Refinery29, December 28, 2017, http://www.refinery29.com/2017/12/184496/amazo-alexa-personality-me-too-era.

35. For example, see Lily Hay Newman, "Turning an Echo into a Spy Device Only Took Some Clever Coding," Wired, April 25, 2018, https://www.wired.com/story/amazon-echo-alexa-skill-spying/. If you read the article (and not just the headline), you'll see why this isn't something to worry about, even though the headline sounds scary.

36. Kieren McCarthy, "Americans Cutting Back on Online Activity over Security and Privacy Fears," Register, May 13, 2016, https://www.theregister.co.uk/2016/05/13/americans_cutting_back_on_online_activity_over_security_and_privacy_fears/. See also "Data Protection Fears Biggest Barrier to Use of Voice Assistants," Research Live, August 29, 2017, https://www.research-live.com/article/news/data-protection-fears-biggest-barrier-to-use-of-voice-assistants/id/5027052.

37. Natt Garun, "How to Set Up Two-Factor Authentication on All Your Online Accounts," Verge, June 17, 2017, https://www.theverge.com/2017/6/17/15772142/how-to-set-up-two-factor-authentication.

Chapter 5

1. Edison Research, "The Infinite Dial 2018," slide 60, March 28, 2018, https://www.slideshare.net/webby2001/infinite-dial-2018/60?src=clipshare.

2. Gartner, "Gartner Reveals Top Predictions for IT Organizations and Users in 2017 and Beyond," press release, October 18, 2016, https://www.gartner.com/newsroom/id/3482117.

3. Gaurav Sharma, "Voice Is the New Platform and the Future of Search, Commerce, and Payments," Chatbots Magazine, July 16, 2016, https://chatbotsmagazine.com/voice-is-the-new-o-s-and-the-future-of-search-commerce-and-payments-64fc8cc848f6.

4. Ibid.; Bernard Marr, "5 Key Artificial Intelligence Predictions for 2018: How Machine Learning Will Change Everything," Forbes, December 18, 2017, https://www.forbes.com/sites/bernardmarr/2017/12/18/5-key-artificial-intelligence-predictions-for-2018-how-machine-learning-will-change-everything/3/.

5. Carolina Milanesi, "Expect to Talk to Your Devices a Lot More in the Future," Recode, January 10, 2018, https://www.recode.net/2018/1/10/16874902/alexa-assistant-voice-activated-amazon-google-interface-bixby-ces-2018.

6. Elizabeth Stinson, "Alexa Is Conquering the World. Now Amazon's Real Challenge Begins," *Wired*, January 18, 2017, https://www.wired.com/2017/01/alexa-conquering-world-now-amazons-real-challenge-begins/.

7. Adam Babajee-Pycroft, "Why Alexa Is More Important Than the iPhone," Natural Interaction, accessed May 15, 2018, https://www.naturalinteraction.com/post/why-alexa-is-more-important-than-the-iphone.

8. Gaurav Sharma, "The Rise of Intelligent 'Voice' Assistants (I.A.)," *Chatbots Magazine*, May 29, 2016, https://chatbotsmagazine.com/intelligent-assistants-i-a-85c21f9d3b8e.

9. Maruti Techlabs, "Cognitive Computing and Why You Need to Know about It," *Chatbots Magazine*, May 30, 2017, https://chatbotsmagazine.com/what-is-cognitive-computing-and-why-you-need-to-know-about-it-6bb2282ebef1.

10. Antonio García Martínez, "The Veni, Vidi, Vici of Voice," *Wired*, February 20, 2018, https://www.wired.com/story/voice-technology-content-commerce/.

11. Sundar Pichai, "This Year's Founders' Letter," *Inside Google*, April 28, 2016, https://blog.google/topics/inside-google/this-years-founders-letter/.

12. James Kobielus, "Everything from Build: Microsoft Drives AI Further into the Edge, Security to the Forefront," Silicon Angle, May 8, 2018, https://siliconangle.com/blog/2018/05/08/everything-build-microsoft-drives-ai-edge-security-forefront/.

13. Yaniv Leviathan and Yossi Matias, "Google Duplex: An AI System for Accomplishing Real-World Tasks over the Phone," *Google AI Blog*, May 8, 2018, https://ai.googleblog.com/2018/05/duplex-ai-system-for-natural-conversation.html.

14. Gaurav Sharma, "Voice Is the New Platform and the Future of Search, Commerce, and Payments," *Chatbots Magazine*, July 16, 2016, https://chatbotsmagazine.com/voice-is-the-new-o-s-and-the-future-of-search-commerce-and-payments-64fc8cc848f6.

15. Amy Nordrum, "CES 2017: The Year of Voice Recognition," *IEEE Spectrum*, January 4, 2017, https://spectrum.ieee.org/tech-talk/consumer-electronics/gadgets/ces-2017-the-year-of-voice-recognition.

16. Kevin Maney, "Alexa, Google Home and Smartphones Could Make Illiteracy Unimportant," *Newsweek*, September 9, 2017, http://www.newsweek.com/2017/09/22/alexa-google-home-smart-phones-illiteracy-technology-voice-recognition-662282.html.

17. Pete Pachal, "Digital Assistants Just Took a Big Step toward Real 'Human' Conversation," Mashable, April 20, 2018, https://mashable.com/2018/04/19/microsoft-xiaoice-full-duplex-voice/#aL0Zac7Ppsqp.

18. Will Knight, "How Uncertainty Could Help a Machine Hold a More Eloquent Conversation," *MIT Technology Review*, May 7, 2018, https://www.technologyreview.com/s/611078/how-uncertainty-could-help-a-machine-hold-a-more-eloquent-conversation/.

19. "How Does Speech Recognition Technology Work?" *Globalme*, March 21, 2018, https://www.globalme.net/blog/how-does-speech-recognition-technology-work.

20. Leor Grebler, "Voice Technology That's More Human Than Human," *IoT for All*, March 9, 2018, https://www.iotforall.com/future-ai-voice-technology/.

21. Search for jobs containing the word "Alexa" at https://www.amazon.jobs/.

22. George Anders, "Alexa, Understand Me," *MIT Technology Review*, August 9, 2017, https://www.technologyreview.com/s/608571/alexa-understand-me/.

23. Gaurav Sharma, "Voice Is the New Platform and the Future of Search, Commerce, and Payments," *Chatbots Magazine*, July 16, 2016, https://chatbotsmagazine.com/voice-is-the-new-o-s-and-the-future-of-search-commerce-and-payments-64fc8cc848f6.

24. Matt Enis, "Voice Activated | Technology in Focus," *Library Journal*, April 2, 2018, https://lj.libraryjournal.com/2018/04/technology/voice-activated-technology-focus; "Introducing the 'LibraryThing Alexa Skill," *Library Thing Blog*, March 12, 2018, http://blog.librarything.com/main/2018/03/introducing-the-librarything-alexa-skill/.

25. Jay Stanley, "The Privacy Threat from Always-On Microphones like the Amazon Echo," *ACLU Blog*, January 13, 2017, https://www.aclu.org/blog/privacy-technology/privacy-threat-always-microphones-amazon-echo.

26. See Chapter 7, "Experimenting," in Nicole Hennig, *Keeping Up with Emerging Technologies: Best Practices for Information Professionals* (Santa Barbara, CA: Libraries Unlimited, 2017).

27. Cosette Jarrett, "Petition Asks Siri and Alexa to Flip the Script on Sexual Harassment," VentureBeat, December 8, 2017, https://venturebeat.com/2017/12/08/petition-asks-siri-and-alexa-to-flip-the-script-on-sexual-harassment/.

Resources

In addition to the sources mentioned in notes throughout this book, here are some of the best sources for keeping up with voice computing.

Blogs and Newsletters

Voicebot.ai: https://www.voicebot.ai/
Love My Echo: https://lovemyecho.com/
Alexa Blogs: https://developer.amazon.com/blogs/alexa/
IoT for All: http://iotforall.com
Hearing Voices Newsletter: https://www.getrevue.co/profile/hearingvoices

News

You can find many useful stories about voice computing on Medium.com by using the following tags:

Alexa: https://medium.com/tag/alexa
Amazon Echo: https://medium.com/tag/amazon-echo
Google Home: https://medium.com/tag/google-home
Siri: https://medium.com/tag/siri
Voice Assistant: https://medium.com/tag/voice-assistant

Discussion Groups

Reddit is a good place to ask questions and see what others are saying about smart speakers:

Google Home: https://www.reddit.com/r/googlehome/
Alexa: https://www.reddit.com/r/alexa/
Amazon Echo: https://www.reddit.com/r/amazonecho/
Siri: https://www.reddit.com/r/Siri/

Statistics

Look for new reports once or twice a year from these sources:

NPR and Edison Research, *The Smart Audio Report*, https://www.nationalpublicmedia.com/smart-audio-report/.

Edison Research, *The Infinite Dial 2018*, March 8, 2018, http://www.edisonresearch.com/infinite-dial-2018/.

Voicebot.ai, *Smart Speaker Consumer Adoption Report 2018*, https://www.voicebot.ai/download-smart-speaker-consumer-adoption-report-2018/. You'll need to submit your email address to download the report.

Design and User Experience of Voice Interfaces

One of the best books available for learning about user interface design for voice is Cathy Pearl's *Designing Voice User Interfaces: Principles of Conversational Experiences* (Sebastopol, CA: O'Reilly Media, 2016), http://shop.oreilly.com/product/0636920050056.do. See also her website: https://www.cathypearl.com/; follow her on Twitter for useful information about voice computing: https://twitter.com/cpearl42.

Speech Recognition and the Handling of Foreign Languages

The company Globalme has a wealth of useful information on its blog: https://www.globalme.net/blog. They cover the basics of speech recognition technology and language support in voice computing. The following articles are good starting points:

"Speech Recognition Technology Overview: A Complete Guide to Speech Recognition Technology," March 12, 2018, https://www.globalme.net/blog/the-present-future-of-speech-recognition.

"Language Support in Voice Assistants Compared," April 13, 2018, https://www.globalme.net/blog/language-support-voice-assistants-compared.

"Innovative Uses of Speech Recognition Today," March 7, 2018, https://www.globalme.net/blog/new-technology-in-speech-recognition.

"OOBE: How Well Does Alexa Handle Accents?" March 12, 2018, https://www.globalme.net/blog/how-well-does-alexa-handle-accents.

Index

About the Author

NICOLE HENNIG is an expert in emerging technologies for libraries. In her 14 years of experience at the MIT Libraries, first as web manager and then as head of user experience, she won awards for innovation and worked to keep academics up to date with the best mobile technologies. In 2013, she left MIT to start her own business helping librarians stay current with new technologies.

She is the author of several books, including *Keeping Up with Emerging Technologies: Best Practices for Information Professionals*. See her publications at http://nicolehennig.com/books and online courses at http://nicolehennig.com/courses.

Nicole enjoys teaching, presenting, and inspiring people to use technology effectively. To stay current with the best new technologies, sign up for her email newsletter, *Mobile Apps News*, at http://nicolehennig.com.